I0489919

1.

2.

3.

4.

5.

6.

7.

8.

9.

10.

11.

12.

13.

PERSONAL FINANCE FOR TEENS
SACHIN BANSODE
Copyright © Sachin Bansode
All Rights Reserved.

Made with ❤ on the Notion Press Platform
www.notionpress.com
To all the amazing youth of India out there.

This book is dedicated to you! Your energy, creativity, and curiosity inspire me every day. I wrote "Stock Market for Teens" because I believe that you deserve to have the knowledge and tools to invest in your future. And now, with "Personal Finance for Teens," I want to help you take control of your finances and build a secure financial future.

In these pages, you'll find practical advice, real-world examples, and easy-to-understand explanations of all the key personal finance concepts you need to know. From budgeting and saving to credit and debt, I'll guide you through everything you need to know to make smart financial decisions.

As a teenager, you're at a unique point in your life, with so many possibilities and opportunities ahead of you. With the knowledge and skills you'll gain from this book, you'll be able to make informed decisions about your money, so that you can achieve your goals and build the life you want.

So, whether you're just starting out on your financial journey or you're looking to take your skills to the next level, I hope you'll find this book informative, engaging, and inspiring. Let's get started!

14.

15.

16.

17.

18.

19.

20.

21.

Foreword

Managing personal finances can be intimidating and overwhelming for anyone, let alone youngsters who are just starting to navigate the complexities of adulthood. However, the importance of developing good financial habits cannot be overstated. By building a solid foundation in personal finance, you can develop the skills and knowledge one needs to achieve their goals, pursue their passions, and build a bright future.

That's why I'm thrilled to introduce "Personal Finance for Teens: Empowering You to Take Control of your Financial Future", written by Sachin. This book provides practical guidance, actionable advice, and easy-to-understand explanations of personal finance concepts that everyone should know.

From budgeting and saving to investing and credit, this book covers all the essential aspects of personal finance. Sachin's engaging writing style, real-life examples, and relatable anecdotes make it easy for the youth to learn and understand these important concepts.

As a professionnal who has worked with many young people, I have seen firsthand the positive impact that financial literacy can have on a person's life. With this book, the author provides a valuable resource for teenagers who are looking to take control of their finances and build a secure financial future.

I highly recommend "Personal Finance for Teens" to teenagers, parents, and educators alike. It is an essential guide that will help teenagers develop the skills and knowledge they need to make informed financial decisions and achieve their goals. Congratulations to Sachin for creating such an informative and engaging book!

Suchith .P.S

Banking professional

Preface

Personal finance can be a daunting topic, especially for teenagers who are just starting to take control of their finances. But as someone who has spent years working with young people, I know that financial literacy is essential for achieving financial independence and building a bright future.

That's why I wrote "Personal Finance for Teens: Empowering You to Take Control of Your Financial Future." This book is designed to be a comprehensive guide that covers all the key aspects of personal finance, from budgeting and saving to investing and credit.

I've worked hard to make this book accessible, engaging, and informative. Each chapter is filled with practical advice, real-world examples, and easy-to-understand explanations of important financial concepts.

But this book is not just for teenagers. Parents, educators, and anyone who cares about the financial future of young people will also find it to be a valuable resource. By reading this book together with the teenagers in your life, you can start important conversations about money management and help them develop the skills and knowledge they need to succeed.

I hope that this book will serve as a helpful guide for teenagers as they navigate the often-confusing world of personal finance. Whether you're just starting out on your financial journey or looking to improve your skills and knowledge, "Personal Finance for Teens" is here to help you take control of your financial future.

Acknowledgements

Writing a book is never a solitary endeavor. There are always many people who contribute their time, expertise, and support to make it happen. I am grateful to all of the individuals who helped make "Personal Finance for Teens" a reality.

First and foremost, I want to thank my family and friends for their unwavering support throughout this journey. Your encouragement, advice, and understanding have been invaluable.

I also want to express my gratitude to the many teachers, educators, and mentors who have inspired me over the years. Your passion for education and dedication to helping young people succeed has motivated me to write this book..

Last but certainly not least, I want to thank the readers who have chosen to pick up this book. It is my hope that the information and advice provided in these pages will help you take control of your financial future and achieve your goals. Your interest and support mean the world to me.

Thank you all from the bottom of my heart.

Prologue

Money. It's something that we all need to survive and thrive in this world. But for many teenagers, money can be a source of stress, anxiety, and confusion. Whether you're trying to save up for a new phone, planning for college, or just trying to make ends meet, managing your personal finances can be a daunting task.

That's why I wrote this book: "Personal Finance for Teens: Empowering Teens to Take Control of Their Financial Future." I wanted to provide a comprehensive guide that would help teenagers navigate the often-confusing world of personal finance, so that they can achieve their goals and build the future they deserve.

Throughout this book, I'll be sharing practical advice, real-world examples, and easy-to-understand explanations of personal finance concepts that every teenager should know. From budgeting and saving to investing and credit, we'll cover all the essential aspects of personal finance.

But this book is more than just a guide to money management. It's also a call to action. It's a reminder that you have the power to take control of your financial future, no matter what your current situation may be. By developing good financial habits and making informed decisions, you can create a secure and prosperous future for yourself.

So if you're ready to take the first step on your financial journey, let's get started. Together, we can empower youth to take control of their financial future and build the lives that our country deserves.

CHAPTER ONE

Introduction to Personal Finance

Welcome, to the world of personal finance! Now, before you start snoring, let's get one thing straight: personal finance doesn't have to be boring. In fact, it can be very interesting! Don't believe me? Well, let me tell you a story about a man who invested in the stock market and lost all his money.

Once upon a time, I had a friend named John who wanted to invest in the stock market and had put his pocket money into it. He was so excited and overconfident that he bought shares in a company called Blockbuster. Now, for those of you who don't know, Blockbuster used to be a video rental store in USA. But with the rise of streaming services like Netflix, Blockbuster went bankrupt. And poor John lost all his money!

Now, I'm not telling you this story to scare you. Instead, I want to show you that personal finance is important, and making wise financial decisions can prevent you from making mistakes like poor John. So, let's dive into the basics.

Personal finance is all about managing your money. Whether you're earning pocket money from chores or working a part-time job, you need to learn how to make the most of your money. And the first step is creating a budget.

Think of a budget as a roadmap for your money. It helps you keep track of your income and expenses and ensures that you're not overspending. Trust me, you don't want to be that kid who blew all their money on the latest iPhone and can't afford to go out with friends.

Budgeting can be fun too! You can think of it as a puzzle where you have to make all the pieces fit. You can challenge yourself to find creative ways to save money, like taking a bus or train instead of Uber

In this book, we'll cover all the basics of personal finance, from budgeting to investing to retirement planning. And we'll do it in a fun and engaging way, with plenty of examples and trivia to keep you entertained. So, get ready to become a personal finance pro and never end up like poor John!

One key aspect is understanding the difference between needs and wants.

Needs are things that are essential for survival, like food, clothing and shelter.

Wants, on the other hand, are things that are nice to have but not necessary for survival, like the latest gaming console or branded clothes.

It's important to prioritize your needs over your wants and not let your wants drain your bank account. Trust me, I know how tempting it can be to splurge on the latest trends, but you don't want to end up broke before the next allowance or paycheck arrives.

Another important concept in personal finance is compound interest. This may sound boring, but trust me, it's one of the most powerful tools in building long-term wealth. Compound interest means earning interest on your initial investment as well as the interest earned over time. The earlier you start investing, the more time your money has to grow through compound interest.

Let's say you invest Rs1000 in a mutual fund at the age of 18 and leave it untouched until you retire at 65. Assuming a 7% annual rate of return, your investment will grow to almost Rs 30,000! That's a 30 X of your invested capital. That's the power of compound interest.

Lastly, I want to stress on the importance of starting early with personal finance. The habits you form now will stick with you for the rest of your life. By starting to budget, save, and invest early, you'll be setting yourself up for a financially stable future.

Now, let's take a closer look at credit and debt.

Credit is borrowing money with the promise to pay it back later, usually with interest. A common form of credit is a credit card, which allows you to make purchases now and pay later. However, credit cards can also be a trap if not used responsibly. If you don't pay your balance in full each month, you'll be charged interest, which can add up quickly.

Debt is when you owe money to someone else. This can include credit card debt, student loans, car loans, and home loans. While some debt can be good, like a loan on a house, too much debt can be harmful to your financial health.

To avoid debt traps, it's important to develop good credit habits. This includes paying your bills on time, keeping your credit utilization low, and avoiding unnecessary debt.

Now, let's switch gears and talk about investing. Investing is the process of putting money into something with the hope of earning a profit. This can include stocks, bonds, mutual funds, and real estate.

While investing can seem intimidating, it's important to start early and do your research. You don't have to be a stock market expert to invest wisely. There are plenty of resources available, such as financial advisors and online investing platforms, that can help you make informed decisions.

Next, I want to emphasize the importance of setting financial goals. What do you want to achieve with your money? Whether it's saving for a car, paying for college, or retiring comfortably, having a clear goal in mind can help you make better financial decisions and stay motivated to save and invest.

So, how do you set financial goals? Start by thinking about your short-term and long-term aspirations. Short-term goals may include saving for a new phone or a trip with friends, while long-term goals may include saving for college or buying a house.

Once you've identified your goals, make a plan to achieve them. This may include setting a budget, increasing your income through a part-time job, or finding ways to save money on your current expenses. Remember to track your progress and make adjustments as needed.

In conclusion,personal finance can be a fun and exciting journey if you approach it with the right mindset. By understanding the basics of budgeting, needs vs. wants, compound interest, credit and debt, investing, and goal-setting, you'll be well on your way to financial success. So, let's continue on this journey together and discover all the amazing things that personal finance can offer!

I hope this introduction to personal finance has shown you that managing your money can be fun, engaging, and even interesting! And don't worry if you don't know everything yet. That's why I'am here. In the coming chapters, we'll explore each topic in more detail and equip you with the knowledge you need to become a personal finance pro. So, let's get started!

CHAPTER TWO

Setting Financial Goals

In the previous chapter, we talked about the importance of personal finance and how it can help you achieve your dreams. Now, let's dive deeper and talk about setting financial goals.

Setting financial goals is essential to personal finance. It gives you direction, motivates you to save, and helps you make informed decisions. But, how do you set financial goals? And what makes a good financial goal?

To answer those questions, let's start with the basics.

What is a financial goal?

A financial goal is a specific target you set for yourself that relates to your money. It can be anything from saving for a vacation to investing in the stock market. The key is that it's specific, measurable, and achievable.

Why is setting financial goals important?

Setting financial goals is essential for several reasons. First, it gives you direction and purpose. When you have a clear goal in mind, it's easier to stay motivated and focused on your financial journey. Second, it helps you make better decisions. By knowing what you're working towards, you can prioritize your spending and avoid impulse purchases that derail your progress. Finally, setting financial goals gives you a sense of accomplishment. When you reach a goal, it's a great feeling of achievement and a sign that you're on the right track.

So, now that we know what financial goals are and why they're important, let's dive into how to set them.

Step 1: Identify your financial goals

The first step in setting financial goals is to identify what you want to achieve. Start by brainstorming your financial aspirations. Don't limit yourself at this stage. Dream big! Here are some examples to get you started:

Saving for a car

Paying off student loans

Investing in the stock market

Starting a business

Saving for a down payment on a house

Once you've brainstormed your financial goals, prioritize them. Ask yourself which goals are most important to you and which ones you want to achieve first.

Step 2: Make your goals SMART

Now that you've identified your financial goals, it's time to make them SMART. SMART stands for Specific, Measurable, Achievable, Relevant, and Time-bound. Let's break down each of these elements.

Specific: Your goal should be specific and clearly defined. For example, "I want to save Rs20,000 for a down payment on a motorbike."

Measurable: Your goal should be measurable so you can track your progress. For example, "I want to save Rs20,000 in 12 months."

Achievable: Your goal should be realistic and achievable. Don't set a goal that's too lofty and unattainable. For example, if you make Rs5000 a month, it's not realistic to save all Rs20,000 in one month.

Relevant: Your goal should be relevant to your financial situation and personal aspirations. For example, if you don't have a car, it's not relevant to save for a boat.

Time-bound: Your goal should have a deadline so you can stay on track and hold yourself accountable. For example, "I want to save Rs20,000 in 12 months by saving Rs1667 a month."

Step 3: Develop a plan to achieve your goals

Now that you've set your SMART financial goals, it's time to develop a plan to achieve them. This is where budgeting comes in. Budgeting is the process of creating a plan for your money that includes your income, expenses, and savings. It's important to have a budget in place to ensure you're on track to achieve your goals.

Here's a quick quiz to test your knowledge about setting financial goals:

1) Why is setting financial goals important?

a. It gives you direction and purpose.

b. It helps you make better decisions.

c. It gives you a sense of accomplishment.

d. All of the above.

2) What does SMART stand for?

a. Specific, Measurable, Achievable, Relevant, and Time-bound.

b. Simple, Measurable, Achievable, Realistic, and Time-bound.

c. Specific, Measurable, Achievable, Reasonable, and Time-bound.

d. None of the above.

3) Why is budgeting important in achieving your financial goals?

a. It helps you track your income and expenses.

b. It ensures you're on track to achieve your goals.

c. It helps you prioritize your spending.

d. All of the above.

Answers: 1d, 2a, 3d

Congratulations, you've completed the quiz!

Now that you understand the importance of setting financial goals and how to make them SMART, it's time to take action. Start by identifying your financial aspirations, making them SMART, and developing a plan to achieve them through budgeting. Remember, setting financial goals is not only important but also fun! It's like setting challenges for yourself and rewarding yourself when you reach them.

In the next chapter, we'll talk about budgeting in more detail and provide tips to help you get started. So, stay tuned!

CHAPTER THREE

Budgeting Basics

Budgeting is the process of creating a plan to allocate your income towards different expenses and financial goals. It is an essential tool for achieving financial stability and success. In this chapter, we will discuss the basics of budgeting, including how to create a budget, common budgeting methods, and tips for staying on track.

Creating a Budget

The first step in creating a budget is to determine your income. This includes all sources of income, such as your part time salary, side hustles, investment income or simply pocket money. Once you have determined your income, you should subtract your fixed expenses, such as Travel expenses,food expenses and any premium subscriptions. This will give you a clear picture of how much money you have left over to allocate towards discretionary expenses and savings goals.

Next, you should list out all of your discretionary expenses, such as groceries, entertainment, and travel. You should also consider any savings goals you have, such as saving for a down payment on a motorbike or paying off a credit card debt. It's important to be realistic about your expenses and to avoid overspending in any one category.

Common Budgeting Methods

There are several common budgeting methods that you can use to allocate your income towards different expenses and financial goals. Here are a few of the most popular methods:

The 50/30/20 Rule: This rule suggests allocating 50% of your income towards fixed expenses, 30%

towards discretionary expenses, and 20% towards savings goals.

For example, if your monthly income is Rs 50,000, you would allocate Rs 25,000 towards fixed expenses, Rs15,000 towards discretionary expenses, and Rs10,000 towards savings goals.

Envelope Method: This method involves dividing your cash into different envelopes for each expense category. This can help you avoid overspending and keep you on track with your budget.

For example, if you have Rs 15000 for groceries for the month, you would put Rs15000 in an envelope labeled "Groceries". Once the money in the envelope is gone, you cannot spend any more on groceries until the next month.

Zero-Based Budgeting: This method involves allocating every rupee of your income towards a specific expense category or savings goal. This can help you stay on track with your budget and ensure that every rupee is being put towards a purpose.

Let's say your monthly income is Rs35,000, and you want to use zero-based budgeting to allocate your expenses:

Housing - Rs15,000

Transportation - Rs5000

Groceries - Rs5000

Utilities - Rs2500

Entertainment - Rs2500

Clothing - Rs1500

Health and Fitness - Rs1000

Miscellaneous - Rs2500

In this example, you have allocated a total of Rs35,000 towards your monthly expenses. However, you can adjust your expenses based on your current needs and priorities. For instance, you may decide to reduce your entertainment expenses to Rs1000 and allocate the remaining Rs1500 towards your health and fitness expenses. This would result in a new monthly budget:

Housing - Rs15,000

Transportation - Rs5,000

Groceries - Rs5,000

Utilities - Rs2,500

Entertainment - Rs1,000

Clothing - Rs1,500

Health and Fitness - Rs2,500

Miscellaneous - Rs2,500

The new budget is still Rs35000, but the allocation has changed based on your priorities. By applying zero-based budgeting, you can make more informed decisions about where to allocate your money, leading to better financial outcomes.

Tips for Staying on Track

Creating a budget is only the first step towards achieving financial stability and success. Here are a few tips for staying on track with your budget:

1.Review your budget regularly: It's important to review your budget regularly and make adjustments as needed. If you notice that you are overspending in a certain category, you may need to adjust your budget to avoid going over your overall spending limit.

2.Use budgeting tools: There are several budgeting tools or apps available that can help you stay on track with your budget. These tools can help you track your spending, set savings goals, and even automate your savings.

3.Avoid impulse purchases: Impulse purchases can quickly derail your budget. To avoid impulse purchases, consider waiting 24 hours before making any non-essential purchases. This can help you avoid making impulsive decisions and ensure that you are only spending money on things that are truly important to you.

Examples

Let's take a look at a few examples to illustrate how budgeting can help you achieve your financial goals:

Example 1: Paying off debt

Samantha has Rs1,00,000 in credit card debt with an interest rate of 18%. She wants to pay off her debt as quickly as possible, but she's not sure where to start. After creating a budget, Samantha realizes that she can allocate an extra Rs5,000 per month towards her credit card payments. She decides to use the snowball method, which involves paying off the smallest debt first and then using that payment towards the next smallest debt, until all debts are paid off.

Using this method, Samantha pays off her smallest credit card debt of Rs10,000 in the first month. She then adds the Rs500 minimum payment she was making on that debt to the Rs500 she was already allocating towards her credit card payments. This means that in the second month, she can allocate Rs1000 towards her credit card payments. She continues this process until all of her credit card debts are paid off.

By creating a budget and using the snowball method, Samantha is able to pay off her credit card debt in just over two years, saving her thousands of Rupees in interest.

Example 2: Saving for a down payment on a house

Jai and Seema want to buy a house in the next two years. They've been saving for a while, but they're not sure if they're on track to reach their savings goal. After creating a budget, they realize that they can allocate an extra Rs5000 per month towards their down payment savings goal.

Using the 50/30/20 rule, Jai and Seema allocate 20% of their income towards their down payment savings goal. They also decide to use a high-yield savings account to earn more interest on their savings.

After two years of following their budget and consistently saving, Jai and Seema are able to reach their savings goal and buy their dream house.

There are many tools and resources available to help you create and stick to your budget. Here are a few examples:

Budgeting apps - There are many apps available that can help you track your spending and create a budget. Some random options include MoneyManager, Good Budget,and YNAB (You Need a Budget). These apps allow you to link your bank accounts and credit cards, so you can see all of your transactions in one place. They also offer budgeting tools and alerts to help you stay on track.

Budgeting Excel worksheets - If you prefer a more hands-on approach, you can use a budgeting excel worksheet to create your budget. Many financial websites offer free budgeting excel worksheets that you can download and print. These excel worksheets typically include categories for income, expenses, and savings goals.

Online calculators - There are many online calculators available that can help you calculate your budget, such as a debt payoff calculator or a retirement savings calculator. These calculators can help you see how much you need to save each month to reach your financial goals.

Financial advisors - If you need more personalized guidance, you can work with a financial advisor. A financial advisor can help you create a budget and develop a financial plan that is tailored to your specific needs and goals. They can also provide ongoing support and advice as you work towards your financial goals.

Tips for Successful Budgeting

Here are some tips to help you create and stick to your budget:

Start with your income - Before you can create a budget, you need to know how much money you have coming in each month. Make a list of all of your sources of income, including your pocket money, freelance work, and any other sources of income.

Track your expenses - Next, make a list of all of your expenses. This includes fixed expenses, such as rent or fees, as well as variable expenses, such as groceries, dining out, and entertainment. You can use a budgeting app or worksheet to help you track your expenses.

Identify areas where you can cut back - Once you have a clear picture of your income and expenses, look for areas where you can cut back. This might mean reducing your dining out budget, canceling subscriptions you don't use, or negotiating your bills.

Allocate your income - Use the 50/30/20 rule or another budgeting method to allocate your income towards different categories, such as hostel rent, transportation, food, and savings. Make sure to prioritize your savings goals, such as paying off debt or saving for retirement.

Review and adjust regularly - Review your budget regularly to make sure you are staying on track with your goals. Adjust your budget as needed, such as if your income changes or if you have unexpected expenses.

Final Thoughts

Budgeting may seem unimportant at first, but it is an essential tool for achieving financial stability and success. By creating a budget and sticking to it, you can pay off debt, save for the future, and achieve your financial goals. There are many budgeting tools and resources available to help you get started, and it's important to review and adjust your budget regularly to ensure that you are staying on track. With patience and perseverance, you can take control of your finances and build a brighter financial future.

CHAPTER FOUR

Saving Strategies

Now that you have a budget in place, it's time to start thinking about saving strategies. Saving money can be challenging, especially when you're on a tight budget. But there are many ways to save money without sacrificing the things you enjoy. In this chapter, we'll explore some saving strategies that you can use to build your savings and reach your financial goals.

Set Savings Goals

One of the best ways to start saving money is to set specific savings goals. This can help you stay motivated and focused on your savings plan. For example, you might set a goal to save 10% of your income each month or to save a certain amount for a vacation or down payment on a motorbike.

Automate Your Savings

Another effective way to save money is to automate your savings towards investments. This means setting up a recurring transfer from your savings account to your mutual funds each month which would earn returns in long term. By automating your savings, you can make sure that you're putting money aside each month without even thinking about it.

Cut Back on Unnecessary Expenses

One of the easiest ways to save money is to cut back on unnecessary expenses. This might mean canceling subscriptions you don't use or cutting back on dining out. In India, you can save a lot of money by making your own food at home instead of buying it from the local restaurant or ordering online.

Shop Smarter

When it comes to shopping, there are many ways to save money. For example, you can buy in bulk to save money on groceries or wait for sales to purchase big-ticket items. In India, you can also save money by bargaining with shopkeepers. Just remember, haggling is an art form, so be prepared to negotiate like a pro.

Invest in Tax-Saving Schemes

In India, there are several tax-saving schemes that can help you save money on your taxes. For example, you can invest in a Public Provident Fund (PPF) or a National Pension System (NPS) to reduce your tax liability. By taking advantage of these tax-saving schemes, you can keep more money in your pocket.

Use Coupons and Discount Codes

When shopping online, be sure to look for coupons and discount codes that can help you save money on your purchases. In India, you can find many websites and apps that offer discount codes for everything from groceries to travel.

Start a Side Hustle

If you're looking for a way to make extra money, consider starting a side hustle. This might mean starting a small business or freelancing on the side. In India, there are many opportunities for side hustles, such as selling homemade snacks or providing tutoring services.

Take Advantage of Credit Card Rewards

Finally, if you use credit cards, be sure to take advantage of rewards programs. In India, many credit cards offer rewards points that can be redeemed for cash back, travel, or other perks. Just be sure to use your credit cards responsibly and pay off your balance in full each month to avoid high interest charges.

Here are some more honorary mentions for saving strategies in India:

Host a potluck party instead of going out to eat. Not only will you save money on restaurant bills, but you'll also get to try out your friends' cooking skills. Just make sure to avoid the potluck curse, where everyone brings chips and dip.

Use your smartphone to download free coupon apps. You can find coupons for everything from movie tickets to haircuts. Just make sure to read the fine print, as some coupons may have restrictions or expiration dates.

Buy generic brands instead of name brands. In India, many generic brands offer the same quality as name brands at a fraction of the cost. Just remember, not all generics are created equal, so be sure to read reviews before you buy.

Get creative with your leftovers. Instead of letting your leftovers go to waste, try turning them into a new dish. For example, leftover rice can be used to make fried rice, and leftover vegetables can be turned into a delicious soup.

Shop at local markets instead of big supermarkets. Not only will you save money, but you'll also support local businesses. Just be prepared to haggle like a pro, as the vendors may try to inflate their prices.

Saving money doesn't have to be boring or difficult. With the right strategies in place, you can build your savings and reach your financial goals. Whether you're cutting back on unnecessary expenses, shopping smarter, or starting a side hustle, there are many ways to save money in India. So, get creative, have fun, and watch your savings grow!

CHAPTER FIVE

Investing for the Future

Investing may not be on your radar just yet, but it's never too early to start planning for your financial future. Whether you want to save for college, buy a motorbike, or travel the world, investing can help you achieve your goals. In this chapter, we'll explore some investment strategies that you can use to start building your wealth and securing your future.

Know the Basics of Investing

Before you start investing, it's important to understand the basics. Investing involves putting your money into assets that have the potential to grow in value over time. Some popular types of investments include stocks, bonds, mutual funds, and real estate. Each type of investment has its own risk and return profile, so it's important to do your research and choose investments that align with your goals and risk tolerance.

Diversify Your Portfolio

One of the most important investment strategies is diversification. This means spreading your money across different types of assets and sectors to reduce your risk. For example, you might invest in stocks, bonds, and real estate to diversify your portfolio. Diversification can help protect your investments from sudden market changes, making it easier to achieve your long-term goals.

Consider Investing in a ELSS Plan

An ELSS plan is a tax-advantaged savings plan designed to help save on tax laibility. Your money is invested in mutual funds, and the invested amount is tax-exempt upto 1,50,000 This means that you can grow your savings while also reducing your tax liability.This situation would arise only if you are making enough to have a tax liability. Most teenagers would not need this .But hey, you can help your parents by reducing their tax liability if they were to invest in your name.

Use a Robo-Advisor

Robo-advisors are automated investment platforms that use algorithms to create and manage investment portfolios. They are a great option for teens who want to start investing but don't have a lot of experience or time to manage their investments. Robo-advisors offer low fees and can help you stay on track with your investment goals.

Start Small

Investing doesn't have to be expensive. You can start with a small amount of money and gradually increase your investments over time. This can help you build your wealth and confidence as an investor. Apps like Zerodha and Upstox and Groww can help you start investing with as little as Rs 500.

Be Patient

Investing is a long-term game, and it's important to stay invested through market ups and downs. Don't get discouraged if your investments don't grow as quickly as you'd like. Remember, investing is about staying patient and focused on your long-term goals.

Time for some Trivia:

Did you know that actor Ashton Kutcher is also a successful tech investor? He has invested in companies like Airbnb, Uber, and Spotify.

Akshay Kumar: The Bollywood superstar is known for his disciplined approach to money management and has invested in a variety of businesses. He has invested in a fitness chain, a production house, and a mobile gaming company, among other ventures.

Shah Rukh Khan: The "King of Bollywood" is also a savvy investor. He has invested in a cricket team, a film production company, and a digital entertainment platform, among other ventures.

Deepika Padukone: The leading lady of Bollywood is not just an actress but also an entrepreneur and investor. She has invested in a fashion brand, a tech startup, and a sports team, among other ventures.

Aamir Khan: The actor-filmmaker has a keen interest in social entrepreneurship and has invested in several startups that focus on social impact. He has invested in a water purifier company, a waste management startup, and a rural education venture, among other initiatives.

Priyanka Chopra: The actress and former Miss World has invested in a dating app, a beauty brand, and a coding education startup, among other ventures.

Sachin Tendulkar: The cricket legend has invested in several ventures, including a sports management company, a healthcare startup, and a restaurant chain.

He is also a co-owner of the Kerala Blasters football team.

MS Dhoni: The former captain of the Indian cricket team has invested in a number of businesses, including a gym chain, a sports tech startup, and a fashion brand. He is also the co-owner of the Chennaiyin FC football team.

Virat Kohli: The current captain of the Indian cricket team is also an investor. He has invested in a sports tech startup, a fitness chain, and a fashion brand, among other ventures.

Yuvraj Singh: The former cricketer has invested in several businesses, including a healthcare startup, a fashion brand, and a mobile gaming company. He has also started his own investment fund to support early-stage startups.

Sourav Ganguly: The former captain of the Indian cricket team is also an investor and has invested in several ventures, including a sports tech startup and a fantasy sports platform.

These examples show that celebs are not just celebs but can also be savvy investors. They use their wealth and influence to invest in businesses and support new ventures, creating opportunities for themselves and others.

Warren Buffet, one of the most successful investors of all time, bought his first stock at the age of 11!

Investing in your favorite brands can be a fun way to get started with investing. For example, if you love Nike sneakers, you might consider investing in Nike stock.

Investing can be like planting a tree. Just as a tree takes time to grow, your investments will take time to grow as well. But with patience and persistence, your investments can bear fruit over time.

If you are interested in investing in the stock market, I highly encourage you to check out my previous book "Stock Markets for Teens". In that book, I teach everything from the basics of the stock market to advanced investing strategies. You'll learn about the different types of stocks, how to research companies, and how to create a portfolio that aligns with your investment goals. By reading that book, you'll gain the knowledge and confidence you need to start investing in the stock market and take control of your financial future. So, be sure to check it out and start your journey towards becoming a successful investor!

CHAPTER SIX

Understanding Credit and Debt

Credit and debt are two financial terms that are often used interchangeably but have very different meanings. Credit refers to the ability to borrow money or obtain goods or services with the understanding that you will pay for them later. Debt, on the other hand, is the amount of money that you owe to someone else. In this chapter, we will discuss the basics of credit and debt, including the different types of credit, how to manage debt, and how to build good credit.

1: Types of Credit

1.1 Revolving Credit: Revolving credit is a type of credit that allows you to borrow money up to a certain limit and then pay it back over time. This type of credit is often associated with credit cards, where you can use your card to make purchases and then pay the balance over time with interest.

1.2 Installment Credit: Installment credit is a type of credit that allows you to borrow money for a specific purpose, such as a car loan or a mortgage. You pay back the loan in fixed installments over a period of time, usually with interest.

1.3 Open Credit: Open credit is a type of credit that allows you to borrow money for a short period of time, such as a month or a few weeks. This type of credit is often associated with payday loans or cash advances, consumer durable loans which can have high interest rates and fees.

2: Managing Debt

2.1 Understanding Debt-to-Income Ratio: One of the most important factors in managing debt is understanding your debt-to-income ratio. This is the percentage of your income that goes towards paying off debt each month. Ideally, your debt-to-income ratio should be less than 36%, as anything higher can make it difficult to manage your monthly expenses.

2.2 Prioritizing Debt Payments: When you have multiple debts, it's important to prioritize which ones to pay off first. This can be done by focusing on the debts with the highest interest rates or by paying off smaller debts first to gain momentum.

2.3 Creating a Debt Repayment Plan: Creating a debt repayment plan can help you stay on track with paying off your debts. This involves creating a budget and allocating a certain amount each month towards paying off your debts. You can also consider consolidating your debts into one payment to make it easier to manage.

3 .Building Good Credit

3.1 Understanding Credit Scores: Your credit score is a number that reflects your creditworthiness and is based on factors such as your payment history, credit utilization, and length of credit history. Having a good credit score can make it easier to obtain loans and credit in the future.

3.2 Paying Bills on Time: One of the most important factors in building good credit is paying your bills on time. Late payments can negatively impact your credit score and make it more difficult to obtain credit in the future.

3.3 Keeping Credit Utilization Low: Credit utilization refers to the percentage of your available credit that you are currently using. Keeping this percentage low can help improve your credit score and show lenders that you are responsible with credit.

4: Common Credit and Debt Mistakes

4.1 Maxing Out Credit Cards: One common mistake is maxing out credit cards, which can lead to high balances and high interest charges. This can also negatively impact your credit score if your credit utilization is too high.

4.2 Applying for Too Much Credit: Another mistake is applying for too much credit at once, which can lead to multiple hard inquiries on your credit report and negatively impact your credit score.

4.3 Ignoring Credit Reports: Ignoring your credit reports can also be a mistake, as they can contain errors or fraudulent activity that can negatively impact your credit score. It's important to check your credit reports regularly and dispute any errors or fraudulent activity.

5: Credit and Debt Trivia

5.1 Credit Bureau of India Limited (CIBIL): In India, the Credit Bureau of India Limited (CIBIL) is the most popular credit bureau that provides credit reports and scores to lenders. CIBIL scores range from 300 to 900, with higher scores indicating better creditworthiness.

5.2 Credit Card Rewards: Credit card rewards are popular in India, with many credit cards offering rewards such as cashback, discounts, and rewards points for purchases. It's important to use credit card rewards responsibly and avoid overspending just to earn rewards.

5.3 Personal Loan Interest Rates: Personal loan interest rates in India can vary widely, with some lenders offering rates as low as 10% and others offering rates as high as 36%. It's important to shop around and compare rates before taking out a personal loan.

Conclusion:

Credit and debt can be complicated topics, but by understanding the different types of credit, how to manage debt, and how to build good credit, you can make informed decisions about your finances and achieve your financial goals. By avoiding common credit and debt mistakes and staying informed about credit and debt trivia in your local context, you can improve your financial health and achieve long-term financial success.

CHAPTER SEVEN

Building and Maintaining Good Credit

Credit is an important part of your financial life. Having good credit can make it easier to get approved for loans, credit cards, and even apartments or jobs. But building good credit takes time and effort. In addition to the previous chapter, we'll go over the basics of building and maintaining good credit, with plenty of relatable examples and funny anecdotes to help you along the way.

1: Understanding Credit

1.1 What is Credit? Credit is simply the ability to borrow money or access goods or services with the understanding that you'll pay for them later. Credit can come in many forms, including credit cards, consumer durable loans, and home loans.

1.2 Why is Credit Important? Having good credit is important for several reasons. First, it can make it easier to get approved for loans or credit cards with favorable terms and lower interest rates. Second, it can help you establish a financial history that can be useful when applying for business loans. And finally, good credit can help you achieve long-term financial stability and success.

2: Building Good Credit

2.1 Paying Your Credit Card Bills on Time: One of the most important things you can do to build good credit is to pay your bills on time. Late payments can negatively impact your credit score and make it harder to get approved for credit in the future.

2.2 Using Credit Responsibly :Using credit responsibly means only borrowing what you can afford to pay back and keeping your credit utilization low. This means using only a portion of your available credit and paying off your balances in full each month.

2.3 Applying for Credit Sparingly: Applying for too much credit at once can negatively impact your credit score, so it's important to apply for credit sparingly and only when you really need it.

2.4 Establishing a Credit History: Establishing a credit history can be difficult if you're just starting out, but there are several things you can do to get started. One option is to become an authorized user on a parent or guardian's credit card, which can help you build credit without having to take on any debt yourself.

3: Maintaining Good Credit

3.1 Checking Your Credit Report :Checking your credit report regularly can help you catch errors or fraudulent activity that could negatively impact your credit score. You're entitled to get free credit report so be sure to take advantage of this and review your reports regularly.

3.2 Keeping Your Balances Low: Keeping your outstanding balances low is important for maintaining good credit. Ideally, you should aim to use no more than 30% of your available credit.

3.3 Avoiding Credit Card Debt: Credit card debt can be one of the biggest threats to your credit score, so it's important to avoid it whenever possible. If you do have credit card debt, work to pay it off as quickly as possible.

3.4 Using Credit Responsibly :Using credit responsibly is just as important for maintaining good credit as it is for building it. This means only borrowing what you can afford to pay back and paying your bills on time.

4: Credit and Debt scenarios to learn from

4.1 The Credit Card Bill: One day, a man received his credit card bill and was shocked to see that it was over Rs 1,00,000. He called the credit card company to dispute the charges, only to find out that his teenage son had used the card to buy a new gaming console and several games. Lesson learned: keep your credit card out of reach of your children!

4.2 The Personal Loan: A young woman wanted to take out a personal loan to buy a new car. She went to the bank and was told that she was approved for a loan, but when she received the paperwork, she realized that the interest rate was much higher than she had anticipated. She went back to the bank to try to negotiate a lower rate, but the bank refused. Frustrated, she decided to shop around and eventually found a better deal at a different bank. Moral of the story: always shop around for the best rates before taking out a loan.

4.3 The Co-Signer :A young man wanted to buy a car, but didn't have enough credit history to get approved for a loan on his own. His father offered to co-sign on the loan, and the young man was thrilled. However, a few months later, the young man lost his job and was unable to make his car payments. As a result, his father's credit was negatively impacted. Lesson learned: co-signing on a loan can be risky, so only do it if you're confident that the borrower will be able to make the payments.

4.4 The Credit Card Reward: A woman received a credit card offer on e-mail that promised a cash back reward for every purchase. Excited, she applied for the card and started using it for all of her everyday purchases. However, she soon realized that the cash back reward wasn't as generous as she had thought and that the interest rate on the card was quite high. She ended up paying more in interest than she earned in rewards. Lesson learned: read the fine print before signing up for a credit card.

5: Conclusion

Building and maintaining good credit is essential for achieving long-term financial stability and success. By understanding how credit works and following the tips and advice outlined in this chapter, you can establish a strong credit history and avoid the pitfalls of debt and credit problems. Remember, good credit takes time and effort, but it's well worth it in the end.

CHAPTER EIGHT

Managing Debt and Avoiding Debt Traps

Debt is a reality of modern life. Whether it's student loans, credit card debt, or a home loan, most people will carry some form of debt at some point in their lives. While debt can be a useful tool for achieving goals like buying a house or paying for education, it can also be a trap that leads to financial instability and stress. In this chapter, we'll explore how to manage debt effectively and avoid common debt traps.

1: Understanding Debt

1.1 What is Debt? Debt is money borrowed from a lender that must be repaid with interest. There are many types of debt, including credit card debt, personal loans, mortgages, and student loans. When you take on debt, you are essentially borrowing money from the future you. This means that you'll need to have a plan to pay back the money you've borrowed, along with interest.

1.2 Good Debt vs. Bad Debt: Not all debt is created equal. Some debt can be considered "good debt" because it helps you achieve a goal or build wealth over time. Examples of good debt include student loans, which can help you get an education and increase your earning potential, and a home loan, which allows you to buy a home that can appreciate in value over time. However, other forms of debt, such as credit card debt, can be considered "bad debt" because they have high interest rates and don't contribute to your financial wellbeing.

2: Managing Debt

2.1 Creating a Debt Management Plan : If you have debt, it's important to have a plan to manage it effectively. A debt management plan involves setting a budget, prioritizing debt repayment, and negotiating with creditors if necessary. The first step in creating a debt management plan is to identify all of your debts and their interest rates. Next, prioritize your debts based on the interest rate and pay off the debt with the highest interest rate first. Finally, consider negotiating with your creditors for lower interest rates or payment plans that fit your budget.

2.2 Snowball Method: One popular strategy for paying off debt is the snowball method. This involves paying off your smallest debts first and then using the money you were paying on those debts to pay off larger debts. The idea behind the snowball method is that small wins can build momentum and help you stay motivated to pay off your debt.

2.3 Debt Consolidation: Debt consolidation involves taking out a single loan to pay off multiple debts. This can be a useful strategy if you have high-interest debt, such as credit card debt. However, it's important to be cautious when considering debt consolidation, as it can sometimes lead to even more debt if you're not careful.

2.4 Top up on a home loan: A top up loan on your house loan can be a better option compared to getting a new car or personal loan because it usually comes with lower interest rates. Since the loan is secured against your home, it poses less risk to the bank, and they may be willing to offer you more favorable rates than with unsecured loans. Additionally, when you take out a top up loan on your house loan, the bank doesn't usually ask for the purpose of the loan. This means that you can use the funds for anything you need, whether it's to purchase a car, renovate your home or pay off other debts. Overall, a top up loan on your house loan can be a smart choice if you're looking to borrow money at a low cost and have equity in your home.

3: Avoiding Debt Traps

3.1 High-Interest Credit Cards One of the most common debt traps is high-interest credit card debt. Credit cards can be a useful tool for building credit and earning rewards, but they can also be a trap if you're not careful. If you're carrying a balance on your credit card, make a plan to pay it off as soon as possible, and consider switching to a lower-interest card if possible.

3.2 Payday Loans Payday loans are short-term loans with extremely high interest rates. They are often used by people who are struggling financially and need money quickly. However, payday loans can be a debt trap because they often lead to a cycle of debt that's hard to break. If you're considering a payday loan, it's important to understand the high interest rates and fees involved and explore other options first.

3.3 Overspending

Overspending is a common problem that many people face. It happens when you spend more than you earn, and it can lead to a buildup of debt. Overspending can be caused by many things, such as peer pressure, keeping up with the Joneses, or just plain old impulse buying.

To avoid overspending, it is important to create a budget and stick to it. Be realistic about your expenses, and don't forget to include things like entertainment, dining out, and other non-essential items. Make sure to set aside some money for savings each month as well.

If you find that you are consistently overspending, it may be time to re-evaluate your lifestyle and make some changes. Perhaps you need to cut back on certain expenses, or maybe you need to find a way to increase your income. Whatever the case may be, it is important to take action before your debt becomes unmanageable.

3.4 Seek Professional Help

If you find yourself struggling to manage your debt and keep up with payments, consider seeking professional help. This could involve speaking to a financial counselor or credit counselor who can provide you with personalized advice and a debt management plan. They can also help you negotiate with creditors to lower your interest rates or work out a payment plan.

Additionally, if you feel like your debt is spiraling out of control and you cannot make payments, you may need to consider filing for bankruptcy. While this should always be a last resort, it can provide relief from overwhelming debt and a fresh start to rebuild your financial life.

4.Understanding Credit Scores

Your credit score is a three-digit number that reflects your creditworthiness and ability to repay debt. Lenders and creditors use your credit score to evaluate your credit risk when deciding whether to approve you for credit and what interest rate to charge.

Your credit score is calculated based on several factors, including:

4.1 Payment history: whether you have made payments on time

4.2 Credit utilization: how much of your available credit you are using

4.3 Length of credit history: how long you have had credit accounts open

4.4 Types of credit: the mix of credit accounts you have, such as credit cards, loans, and mortgages

4.5 New credit: how often you apply for new credit accounts

Credit scores range from 300 to 850, with higher scores indicating better creditworthiness. A good credit score is typically considered to be above 700.

5). Building and Maintaining Good Credit

Building and maintaining good credit is essential to achieving financial success. Here are some tips to help you build and maintain good credit:

5.1 Make Payments on Time

Paying your bills on time is the most important factor in building and maintaining good credit. Late payments can negatively impact your credit score and stay on your credit report for up to seven years. Set up automatic payments or reminders to ensure you never miss a payment.

5.2 Keep Credit Utilization Low

Credit utilization refers to how much of your available credit you are using. Keeping your credit utilization low (below 30%) shows lenders that you are responsible with credit and can help improve your credit score.

5.3 Limit New Credit Applications

While having a mix of credit accounts is important, applying for new credit accounts frequently can be viewed as a sign of financial instability. Limit new credit applications and only apply for credit when you need it.

5.4 Monitor Your Credit Report

Monitoring your credit report regularly can help you detect and correct errors or fraudulent activity. You can get a free copy of your credit report once a year from each of the three major credit bureaus.

6)Managing Debt and Avoiding Debt Traps

Managing debt can be challenging, but it is important to stay on top of your payments and avoid falling into debt traps. Here are some tips to help you manage debt and avoid debt traps:

6.1 Prioritize High-Interest Debt

Focus on paying off high-interest debt first to save money on interest charges. This may involve making extra payments or consolidating debt with a lower interest rate loan.

6.2 Avoid Minimum Payments

Paying only the minimum payment on credit cards can keep you in debt for years and cost you thousands in interest charges. Always aim to pay more than the minimum payment, even if it is just a little bit.

6.3 Beware of Debt Settlement or Debt Relief Scams

Be wary of companies that offer to settle your debt for pennies on the dollar or promise to eliminate your debt completely. These are often scams that can leave you in a worse financial situation.

6.4 Consider Credit Counseling

If you are struggling to manage your debt, consider seeking credit counseling. A credit counselor can help you create a budget and debt management plan and

CHAPTER NINE

Understanding Taxes and How to File Them

Taxes are an inevitable part of life, but they don't have to be boring or confusing. In fact, understanding taxes can be a fun and interesting way to learn about personal finance. As a teenager, you may not have to file taxes just yet, but it's important to have a basic understanding of how taxes work and how to file them correctly when the time comes. In this chapter, we'll explore the world of taxes and provide you with a fun and interactive guide to understanding and filing taxes.

Section 1: What are Taxes?

Taxes are fees that individuals and businesses pay to the government to support public services such as roads, schools, and hospitals. Taxes can be levied on various sources of income, such as wages, salaries, investments, and property. In India, taxes are divided into two broad categories: direct taxes and indirect taxes.

Direct taxes are taxes that are paid directly by individuals or businesses to the government. These include income tax, corporate tax, and wealth tax. Indirect taxes, on the other hand, are taxes that are paid indirectly by individuals or businesses when they purchase goods or services. These include goods and services tax (GST), customs duty, and excise duty.

Quiz:

What are taxes?

a. Fees that individuals and businesses pay to the government to support public services

b. Fees that individuals and businesses pay to private companies

c. Fees that individuals and businesses pay to charities

What are the two broad categories of taxes in India?

a. Direct taxes and indirect taxes

b. National taxes and state taxes

c. Personal taxes and business taxes

Section 2: Income Tax

Income tax is a direct tax that is levied on the income of individuals and businesses. In India, income tax rates vary depending on the income bracket of the taxpayer. The income tax system in India is progressive, which means that the more you earn, the higher your tax rate. The income tax department issues a form called the Income Tax Return (ITR) that individuals must fill out and file with the government.

Example:

Rohan is a 19-year-old college student who works part-time at a local restaurant. He earns Rs. 1,50,000 per year. According to the income tax rules in India, Rohan is not required to pay income tax because his income falls below the taxable limit. However, he still needs to file an ITR to claim any tax refund he may be eligible for.

Exercise:

Calculate the income tax for the following scenarios as per old and new regimes:

Scenario 1: Priya earns Rs. 3,00,000 per year.
Scenario 2: Rahul earns Rs. 10,00,000 per year.

Section 3: Goods and Services Tax (GST)

Goods and services tax (GST) is an indirect tax that is levied on the sale of goods and services. In India, GST was introduced in 2017 to replace multiple indirect taxes such as excise duty, service tax, and value-added tax (VAT). The GST system in India is divided into four categories: 5%, 12%, 18%, and 28%.

Trivia:

What is the highest GST rate in India?

a. 5% b. 12% c. 18% d. 28%

Section 4: How to File Taxes

Filing taxes can seem confusing, but it's a relatively straightforward process once you understand the basics. In India, taxpayers can file their taxes online or offline. To file taxes online, individuals must register on the Income Tax Department website and follow the instructions to fill out and submit their tax return. To file taxes offline, individuals can download the tax form from the Income Tax Department website, fill it out, and submit it physically to the designated tax office.

Exercise:

Let's practice filing taxes! Download the ITR form from the Income Tax Department website and fill it out for the following scenario:

Scenario: You are a 17-year-old high school student who earned Rs. 50,000 from a summer job. You have no other sources of income. According to the income tax rules in India, your income is below the taxable limit. However, you still need to file an ITR to claim any tax refund you may be eligible for.

Section 5: Common Tax Deductions

Tax deductions are expenses that can be subtracted from your taxable income, reducing the amount of tax you owe. In India, there are several common tax deductions that individuals can claim, such as medical expenses, charitable donations, and education expenses.

Example:

Sonia is a 16-year-old student who donates Rs. 10,000 to a local charity. She can claim this donation as a tax deduction when she files her taxes.

Quiz:

What is the maximum amount of tax deduction allowed for charitable donations in India?

a. 10% of taxable income

b. 15% of taxable income

c. 20% of taxable income

d. 25% of taxable income

Section 6: Penalties for Late Filing

Filing taxes late can result in penalties and fines. In India, taxpayers who file their taxes after the due date can be charged a penalty of up to Rs. 5,000. However, as a relief to small taxpayers, the IT department has stated that if your total income is not more than Rs 5 lakh, the maximum penalty levied for delay will only be Rs.1,000.

Example:Raj is a 18-year-old college student who forgets to file his taxes on time. He is charged a penalty of Rs. 1,000 for filing his taxes late since his income is well below Rs 5,00,000.

Quiz:

What are tax deductions?

a. Expenses that can be subtracted from your taxable income, reducing the amount of tax you owe

b. Additional taxes that must be paid on top of the regular tax

c. Fees charged for filing taxes

What is the penalty for late filing of taxes in India?

a. Up to Rs. 5,000

b. Up to Rs. 10,000

c. Up to Rs 20,000

Section 7: Tax Saving Investments

In India, there are several tax-saving investment options available to individuals, such as Public Provident Fund (PPF), Equity-Linked Savings Scheme (ELSS), National Pension Scheme (NPS), and more. These investments not only help individuals save on taxes but also provide long-term benefits such as wealth creation and financial stability.

Example:

Ankit is a 19-year-old college student who has a part-time job. He invests Rs. 50,000 in an ELSS mutual fund to save on taxes. As a result, he is able to claim a tax deduction of Rs. 50,000 when he files his taxes.

Trivia:

What is the maximum amount that can be invested in PPF in a financial year?

a. Rs. 1 lakh

b. Rs. 1.5 lakhs

c. Rs. 2 lakhs

d. Rs. 2.5 lakhs

Section 8: Common Mistakes to Avoid

Filing taxes can be a daunting task, especially for first-time filers. Here are some common mistakes that individuals should avoid when filing taxes:

Failing to report all sources of income

Forgetting to claim deductions and exemptions

Filing taxes with incorrect personal information

Filing taxes late or not at all

Example:

Sarika is a 18-year-old high school student who earned Rs. 25,000 from a part-time job. However, she forgets to report this income when she files her taxes. As a result, she is charged a penalty for under-reporting her income.

Quiz:

What are some common tax-saving investments in India?

a. Savings account

b. Real estate

c. National Pension Scheme

d. All of the above

What is a common mistake to avoid when filing taxes?

a. Reporting all sources of income

b. Filing taxes late

c. Forgetting to claim deductions and exemptions

Conclusion:

Understanding taxes may not be the most exciting topic, but it's an important part of personal finance. By learning the basics of taxes, you can save money and avoid penalties. Plus, knowing how to file taxes correctly can give you a sense of independence and responsibility. So don't be intimidated by taxes – embrace them as a fun and interesting way to learn about personal finance!

CHAPTER TEN

Smart Spending Habits

When it comes to personal finance, it's not just about earning money, but also about how we spend it. Smart spending habits are crucial for maintaining financial stability and achieving our financial goals. In this chapter, we'll explore some practical tips and tricks for spending money wisely.

Setting Financial Goals

Before we dive into the specifics of smart spending habits, it's important to set financial goals. This could be anything from saving for a vacation to buying a car or saving for retirement. Setting clear financial goals helps us prioritize our spending and avoid impulsive purchases.

Example:

Raj is a 17-year-old high school student who wants to save money for higher studies. He sets a goal of saving Rs. 1 lakh in the next two years. This goal helps him prioritize his spending and avoid unnecessary expenses.

Quiz:

Why is it important to set financial goals?

a. To prioritize spending

b. To avoid impulsive purchases

c. To achieve financial stability

d. All of the above

Tracking Expenses

One of the most effective ways to control our spending is by tracking our expenses. This means keeping track of every rupee we spend and categorizing it into different expenses such as groceries, entertainment, transportation, etc.

Example:

Sneha is a 16-year-old high school student who wants to start tracking her expenses. She starts by writing down every rupee she spends and categorizing it into different expenses. This helps her identify areas where she can cut back on spending.

Trivia:

What are some popular budgeting apps in India?

a. MoneyControl

b. ETMoney

c. Walnut

d. All of the above

Budgeting

Once we've tracked our expenses, the next step is to create a budget. A budget is a plan for how we'll spend our money in the coming days or months. It helps us prioritize our spending and avoid overspending.

Example:

Varun is a 19-year-old college student who creates a budget of Rs. 4,000 for the month. He divides this budget into different expenses such as rent, food, transportation, and entertainment. This helps him stay within his means and avoid overspending.

Quiz:

What is the purpose of creating a budget?

a. To prioritize spending

b. To avoid overspending

c. To achieve financial goals

d. All of the above

How can tracking expenses help with budgeting?

a. It helps identify areas where we can cut back on spending

b. It helps us prioritize spending

c. It helps us achieve financial goals

d. All of the above

Saving Money

Smart spending habits also include finding ways to save money. This could be anything from using coupons and discounts to buying second-hand items or shopping during sales.

Example:

Arun is a 20-year-old college student who wants to save money on groceries. He starts using coupons and buying generic brands instead of branded items. This helps him save money without compromising on quality.

Trivia:

What is a common way to save money on transportation?

a. Taking a taxi

b. Buying a car

c. Using public transportation

d. Walking

Avoiding Impulse Purchases

One of the biggest challenges of smart spending habits is avoiding impulse purchases. Impulse purchases are purchases we make on a whim without thinking about their long-term consequences. To avoid impulse purchases, it's important to think about whether we really need the item and how it fits into our budget.

Example:

Neha is a 18-year who just started college. She's excited to be on her own and wants to make the most of her newfound independence. However, she also wants to make sure she doesn't end up broke by the end of the semester.

Neha's parents have given her a budget for her living expenses, but she's finding it difficult to stick to it. She's tempted by all the new experiences and opportunities that college has to offer, and she doesn't want to miss out on anything.

If you can relate to Neha's situation, don't worry – you're not alone. Learning how to manage your money and make smart spending decisions takes time and practice. But with a few tips and tricks, you can avoid common money mistakes and make your money go further.

Here are some things to keep in mind when it comes to smart spending habits:

Prioritize your expenses: Before you start spending your money, think about what's most important to you. Do you need to pay for rent, groceries, and other essentials first, or do you want to splurge on something fun? Make a list of your expenses and rank them in order of importance.

Avoid impulse purchases: It's easy to get caught up in the moment and buy something you don't really need. Before making a purchase, take a few minutes to think it over. Do you really need it? Can you afford it? Is there a better use for your money?

Set a budget: Just like with saving, setting a budget for your spending can help you stay on track. Determine how much you can afford to spend each week or month and stick to it. Use budgeting apps or spreadsheets to track your expenses and make adjustments as needed.

Look for deals and discounts: There are plenty of ways to save money on things you need or want. Look for coupons, discounts, and sales before making a purchase. You can also try buying things secondhand or borrowing from friends.

Avoid credit card debt: Credit cards can be a useful tool for building credit and earning rewards, but they can also lead to debt if not used responsibly. Try to pay off your balance in full each month and avoid making purchases you can't afford to pay off.

Now, let's put your knowledge to the test with a fun quiz!

What should you do before making an impulse purchase?

a) Buy it right away

b) Think it over for a few minutes

c) Ask your friends for their opinion

What's a good way to save money on purchases?

a) Always buy new items

b) Look for coupons and discounts

c) Pay full price

How can you avoid credit card debt?

a) Only pay the minimum payment each month

b) Make purchases you can't afford

c) Pay off your balance in full each month

Answers: 1) b, 2) b, 3) c.

Congratulations, you're on your way to becoming a smart spender! Remember, managing your money is all about balance. It's okay to treat yourself once in a while, but make sure you're also taking care of your needs and saving for your future. Keep practicing these smart spending habits and you'll be well on your way to financial success.

CHAPTER ELEVEN

Building a Strong Financial Foundation

As a teenager, you may not have a lot of money to work with, but you can still build a strong financial foundation for your future. Creating good financial habits now will help you be successful later in life. In this chapter, we will discuss how to build a strong financial foundation and set yourself up for success.

Budgeting

The first step to building a strong financial foundation is to create a budget. A budget is a plan for how you will spend your money. It should include all of your income and expenses, including money you receive from allowances, part-time jobs, or gifts.

Creating a budget is easy. Start by listing all of your sources of income, such as your allowance, part-time job, or gifts. Next, list all of your expenses, such as food, clothes, and entertainment. Finally, subtract your expenses from your income to see how much money you have left over.

If you have money left over, you can use it to save or invest. If you don't have any money left over, you will need to cut back on your expenses or find ways to increase your income.

Saving

Saving is an essential part of building a strong financial foundation. You should aim to save at least 10% of your income, but more is always better. Saving money will help you achieve your goals, such as buying a car or going to college.

To start saving, create a separate savings account and deposit money into it regularly. You can also set up automatic transfers from your checking account to your savings account to make saving easier.

Investing

Investing is another way to build a strong financial foundation. Investing involves putting your money into assets that will grow in value over time, such as stocks, bonds, or real estate.

While investing can be risky, it can also provide significant returns over the long term. To start investing, do your research and consult with a financial advisor. It's important to remember that investing is a long-term strategy, and you should be prepared to ride out any short-term fluctuations in the market.

Managing Debt

Managing debt is another critical part of building a strong financial foundation. While debt can be a useful tool, it can also be a burden if not managed properly. Make sure you understand the terms of any debt you take on, including interest rates, repayment periods, and penalties for late payments.

To manage debt effectively, create a plan to pay it off as quickly as possible. Focus on paying off high-interest debt first, such as credit card debt. You can also consider consolidating your debt or transferring it to a lower interest rate credit card.

Building Credit

Building credit is another essential part of building a strong financial foundation. Good credit is necessary to get approved for loans, credit cards, and even rental agreements. To build credit, start by getting a credit card or loan in your name and make your payments on time.

It's important to be responsible with your credit. Only use your credit card for purchases you can afford to pay off, and make sure you make your payments on time. Avoid maxing out your credit card or taking on too much debt, as this can hurt your credit score.

Planning for the Future

Finally, building a strong financial foundation means planning for the future. Start by setting goals for yourself, such as saving for college or a down payment on a house. Create a plan to achieve these goals, and track your progress regularly.

It's also important to plan for unexpected events, such as a job loss or medical emergency. Build an emergency fund to cover your expenses for at least three to six months in case of an emergency.

Continuing Education

Continuing education is an essential part of building a strong financial foundation. As you enter the workforce, consider pursuing additional education or training to increase your earning potential. This can include attending college or trade school, taking courses or certification programs, or attending workshops or conferences.

Investing in your education can pay off in the long run, as it can lead to higher-paying job opportunities and career advancement. Make sure to research potential career paths and the education and skills needed to succeed in those fields.

Seeking Professional Advice

Seeking professional advice is another critical part of building a strong financial foundation. If you have questions or concerns about your finances, consider consulting with a financial advisor or other professional. They can provide guidance on budgeting, investing, debt management, and other financial topics.

It's important to choose a reputable and trustworthy financial advisor. Look for someone who is licensed and has experience in the areas you need help with. You can also ask for referrals from friends or family members who have worked with a financial advisor.

Avoiding Financial Pitfalls

Avoiding financial pitfalls is essential to building a strong financial foundation. There are many common financial mistakes that you should try to avoid, such as overspending, taking on too much debt, or not saving enough.

It's also important to be wary of scams and fraudulent activity. Never give out personal or financial information to someone you don't know, and always research offers that seem too good to be true.

Reevaluating Your Financial Plan

Finally, building a strong financial foundation requires ongoing evaluation and adjustment. As your financial situation changes, you may need to reevaluate your goals and adjust your plan accordingly. This can include revising your budget, changing your investment strategy, or adjusting your savings goals.

Make sure to regularly review your financial plan and track your progress towards your goals. Celebrate your successes, and don't be afraid to make changes when needed.

Examples:

Budgeting: Creating a budget can help you prioritize your spending and avoid overspending. For example, you can set aside a certain amount each month for groceries, entertainment, and other expenses, and adjust your spending accordingly.

Saving: Starting a savings account can help you build an emergency fund and save up for future expenses. For example, you can set a goal to save a certain amount each month and use that money to pay for a car, vacation, or other big expense.

Investing: Investing in stocks, mutual funds, or other assets can help you grow your wealth over time. For example, you can invest in a company you believe in or a fund that tracks the performance of a particular sector.

Debt management: Managing your debt can help you avoid high interest rates and fees. For example, you can prioritize paying off high-interest debt first and avoid taking on new debt unless necessary.

Credit building: Building your credit score can help you qualify for loans, credit cards, and other financial products with better terms. For example, you can use a credit card responsibly by paying off the balance in full each month and keeping your credit utilization low.

Learning from mistakes: Building a strong financial foundation often involves learning from mistakes. For example, overspending or taking on too much debt can teach you the importance of budgeting and debt management.

Setting goals: Setting financial goals can help you stay motivated and focused. For example, setting a goal to save for a down payment on a house or pay off all of your debt can give you a clear sense of direction.

Seeking advice: Seeking advice from financial professionals or mentors can help you make informed decisions and avoid costly mistakes. For example, consulting with a financial advisor or attending a financial planning workshop can give you valuable insights into managing your money.

Fun trivia:

The highest denomination note in circulation in India is the Rs 2,000 note, which was introduced in 2016 as part of the government's demonetization efforts.

The Reserve Bank of India (RBI) is the central bank of India and is responsible for issuing currency, setting monetary policy, and regulating the banking sector.

The National Pension System (NPS) is a voluntary retirement savings scheme in India that was launched in 2004. It allows individuals to contribute to their retirement savings and receive tax benefits.

The Indian government launched the Pradhan Mantri Jan Dhan Yojana (PMJDY) in 2014, which aims to provide financial inclusion to every household in India by providing access to banking services such as savings accounts, insurance, and pensions.

Conclusion

Building a strong financial foundation takes time, effort, and discipline, but it's well worth the effort. By following these tips, you can set yourself up for a financially stable and successful future. Remember to be patient and persistent, and don't hesitate to seek professional advice when needed. With the right mindset and habits, you can achieve your financial goals and live the life you want.

CHAPTER TWELVE

Paying for Higher Education

Going to college is an important step in building a successful career, but it can also be a significant financial burden. In India, paying for college can be a huge task, especially for those who come from low-income families. In this chapter, we will explore the different ways to pay for college in India and share real-life experiences, trauma, examples, and trivia related to this topic.

Part 1: The Cost of College in India

Attending college in India can be a daunting task, especially when considering the cost associated with it. The expenses of college life are not just limited to tuition fees, but also include accommodation, food, transportation, and other miscellaneous expenses. In this chapter, we will explore the cost of college in India, but with a fun twist. We will include real-life examples, trivia, and humor to make it an enjoyable read.

A: The High Cost of Education in India

In recent years, the cost of education in India has been on the rise, making it difficult for students from low-income families to attend college. According to a report by the National Sample Survey Organization (NSSO), the average annual expenditure on education per student in rural areas is Rs 5,004 ($67) and Rs 12,833 ($172) in urban areas. These costs include tuition fees, textbooks, and other education-related expenses.Rohan, a college student from a middle-class family in Mumbai, had to work part-time to pay for his college expenses. His family struggled to meet the high cost of education, and he had to take on the burden of paying for his own education.

B: The Rising Cost of Tuition Fees

The tuition fees for higher education in India have been increasing steadily, making it difficult for students from low-income families to afford a college education. The increase in tuition fees is due to the rising costs of education, infrastructure, and faculty salaries.

Real-life experience: Priya, a college student from Delhi, had to drop out of college due to the rising cost of tuition fees. Her parents, who were both working-class, could not afford to pay the high fees for her education.

C: The Impact of Inflation on College Expenses

Inflation has a significant impact on the cost of education in India. The rising cost of living makes it difficult for students to afford a college education, especially when inflation is high.

Real-life experience: Naveen, a college student from Bangalore, had to take out an education loan to pay for his college expenses due to inflation. The cost of living had increased, making it difficult for his family to meet the expenses of his education.

D: The Importance of Budgeting for College Expenses

Budgeting is essential for students who want to manage their college expenses effectively. A budget can help students keep track of their expenses, plan for unexpected expenses, and ensure that they do not overspend.

Real-life experience: Ritu, a college student from Hyderabad, learned the importance of budgeting the hard way. She overspent on her college expenses during her first year, and had to rely on part-time jobs to make ends meet during the rest of her college years.

E: Trivia

The first Indian university, the University of Calcutta, was established in 1857.

The Indian Institute of Technology (IIT) in Bombay is known for its beautiful campus, which is often used as a location for Bollywood films.

The Indian Institute of Management (IIM) in Ahmedabad has been ranked as the best management college in India for several years in a row.

The Indian government launched the Pradhan Mantri Jan Dhan Yojana in 2014, which is a financial inclusion program that provides access to banking services to low-income families.

The All India Council for Technical Education (AICTE) is the regulatory body responsible for the accreditation and maintenance of the standards of technical education in India.

Attending college in India can be expensive, but it is also a worthwhile investment in one's future. By budgeting and planning carefully, students can manage the cost of education effectively. While the rising cost of education is a serious issue, it is important to remember that there is still room for fun, humor, and trivia in the midst of it all.

Part 2: Financial Aid and Scholarships

The high cost of attending college in India can be a challenge for many students and their families. However, there are ways to make college more affordable through financial aid and scholarships. In this chapter, we will explore the world of financial aid and scholarships in India, with a focus on real-life examples, trivia, and humor.

A: The Importance of Financial Aid

Financial aid can make college more affordable for students and their families. Financial aid includes grants, scholarships, work-study programs, and loans. These forms of aid can help students cover the cost of tuition fees, books, and other college expenses.

Real-life experience: Anjali, a college student from Chennai, was able to attend college thanks to the financial aid she received from the government. She was awarded a scholarship that covered her tuition fees and other expenses, which made it possible for her to pursue her degree.

B: Types of Financial Aid

There are several types of financial aid available to college students in India. These include:

Government scholarships and grants: These are awarded by the government to students who meet certain criteria, such as academic merit or financial need.

Private scholarships and grants: These are awarded by private organizations, foundations, and companies to students who meet their specific criteria.

Work-study programs: These programs allow students to work on-campus or off-campus to earn money to pay for their college expenses.

Education loans: These are loans offered by banks and other financial institutions to help students pay for their college expenses.

Real-life experience: Arun, a college student from Bangalore, was able to attend college thanks to an education loan he received from a bank. The loan covered his tuition fees, accommodation, and other expenses, which he was able to repay after he graduated and got a job.

C: The Scholarship Application Process

Applying for scholarships can be a time-consuming and challenging process. Students need to research the scholarships they are eligible for, complete the application forms, and submit the required documents. It is essential to start the scholarship application process early and to ensure that all the required documents are submitted on time.

Real-life experience: Pooja, a college student from Mumbai, spent several months researching scholarships and completing the application forms. She was awarded a scholarship that covered her tuition fees and other expenses, which allowed her to focus on her studies without the burden of financial stress.

D: Trivia

The Central Board of Secondary Education (CBSE) offers several scholarships to students who excel in academics, sports, and other areas.

The Jawaharlal Nehru University (JNU) in Delhi is known for its liberal arts programs and social justice initiatives.

The Tata Trusts offer several scholarships to students pursuing higher education in India and abroad.

The Rashtriya Indian Military College (RIMC) in Dehradun is a military school that offers scholarships to students who excel in academics and sports.

The Indian government offers several scholarships to students from low-income families, such as the Post Matric Scholarship and the Pre-Matric Scholarship.

Tips for Successful Scholarship Applications

Here are some tips to help students increase their chances of receiving scholarships:

Start early: Begin researching scholarships as soon as possible to ensure that you have enough time to complete the applications and submit them on time.

Look for scholarships that match your interests: There are scholarships available for a wide range of interests, including sports, music, art, and academics. Find scholarships that match your interests and apply for them.

Keep track of deadlines: Keep a calendar of scholarship deadlines and make sure to submit your applications well before the deadline.

Follow instructions carefully: Make sure to read the scholarship application instructions carefully and follow them closely. Failure to follow instructions can result in disqualification.

Get organized: Keep all of your scholarship application materials organized in one place, including transcripts, recommendation letters and documents.

Rajesh, a college student from Hyderabad, received several scholarships during his time in college by following these tips. He was able to graduate debt-free and pursue his dream career thanks to the financial aid he received.Financial aid and scholarships can make college more affordable for students in India. It is essential for students to research the scholarships and financial aid options available to them and to start the application process early. By following the tips in this chapter, students can increase their chances of receiving financial aid and scholarships and achieve their academic and career goals without the burden of excessive debt.

Part 3: Education Loans

Pursuing higher education can be expensive, and many students in India turn to education loans to fund their studies. In this chapter, we will explore the different types of education loans available in India, the application process, pros and cons, and more.

A: Types of Education Loans

There are two types of education loans available in India: secured and unsecured loans.

Secured loans require students to provide collateral, such as property, as security against the loan. These loans usually have lower interest rates, longer repayment periods, and higher loan amounts. Some examples of secured loans include the State Bank of India's Student Loan Scheme and ICICI Bank's Education Loan.

Unsecured loans do not require collateral but may have higher interest rates and shorter repayment periods. Examples of unsecured loans include the HDFC Bank's Education Loan and Axis Bank's Education Loan.

B: Procedure for Applying for Education Loans

To apply for an education loan, students must follow these steps:

Research the different loan options available and compare their interest rates, repayment periods, and other terms and conditions.

Choose the loan that best fits your needs and eligibility criteria.

Gather all the required documents, such as proof of admission to the educational institution, income tax returns, and identity proof.

Submit the application along with the necessary documents to the chosen bank or financial institution.

Await approval and disbursement of the loan amount.

Real-life experience: Priya, a student from Delhi, wanted to pursue a master's degree in the United States. She applied for an education loan from HDFC Bank and was able to finance her studies with ease. She now works for a multinational corporation and is paying back her loan comfortably.

C: Pros and Cons of Education Loans

Pros:

Education loans provide access to higher education for students who cannot afford it.

Loans can cover not only tuition fees but also living expenses, travel expenses, and other costs associated with studying.

Interest on education loans is tax-deductible under Section 80E of the Income Tax Act.

Education loans can help build a good credit history if repaid on time.

Cons:

Education loans come with interest rates, which can add up to a significant amount over the repayment period.

In case of default, the collateral provided by the student or their family can be seized by the bank.

Students must repay the loan even if they do not complete their studies or do not get a job after completing their studies.

D: Interesting Facts and Trivia

As of March 2021, the outstanding education loan amount in India stood at around Rs. 2.73 lakh crore.

The State Bank of India is the largest provider of education loans in India.

The maximum loan amount for studies in India is usually around Rs. 10 lakh, while it can go up to Rs. 20-30 lakh for studies abroad.

Many banks and financial institutions offer special education loan schemes for students from economically weaker sections and minority communities.

Education loans are an essential tool for students in India to finance their higher education. However, students must weigh the pros and cons carefully before taking on debt. By researching the available loan options and following the application process diligently, students can make informed decisions about their education financing and achieve their academic and career goals

Part 4: Part-time Jobs and Internships

Part-time jobs and internships can be a great way for teens to earn money, gain work experience, and develop new skills. In this chapter, we will explore the benefits of part-time jobs and internships, how to find them, and some examples of successful outcomes.

A: Benefits of Part-time Jobs and Internships

Part-time jobs and internships have several benefits for teens:

Earning Money: Part-time jobs and internships provide teens with a source of income, which can help them become more independent and financially responsible.

Building Work Experience: Part-time jobs and internships help teens develop valuable work experience, which can be used to build their resumes and improve their chances of getting a job in the future.

Developing New Skills: Part-time jobs and internships allow teens to learn new skills, such as time management, communication, and problem-solving.

Networking: Internships can provide opportunities to network with professionals in the field, which can be useful when searching for future job opportunities.

B: Finding Part-time Jobs and Internships

There are several ways teens can find part-time jobs and internships:

Online job search engines: Teens can use job search engines such as Internshala, Naukri, Indeed, Monster, or LinkedIn to search for part-time jobs and internships.

Social media: Teens can use social media platforms such as LinkedIn or Twitter to search for job opportunities and network with professionals in their field of interest.

Local businesses: Teens can visit local businesses in their area and inquire about part-time job opportunities.

Real-life experience: Rahul, a high school student from Mumbai, was interested in pursuing a career in journalism. He found an internship opportunity with a local newspaper and was able to gain valuable experience and build his portfolio. He later used this experience to land a job at a national news organization after graduating from college.

C: Examples of Successful Outcomes

Part-time jobs and internships can lead to successful outcomes for teens:

Professional Development: By gaining work experience, teens can develop their professional skills and become more attractive to potential employers.

College Applications: Part-time jobs and internships can be used to demonstrate a student's work experience and commitment on college applications.

Long-term Career Opportunities: Internships can lead to long-term job opportunities with the organization or company the student interned with.

D: Interesting Facts and Trivia

The most common types of part-time jobs for teens in India include tutoring, retail, and food service.

The minimum age for legal employment in India is 14 years old, but there are restrictions on the types of work minors can do.

Internships can range from a few weeks to several months and can be paid or unpaid.

Part-time jobs and internships can provide valuable opportunities for teens to earn money, gain work experience, and develop new skills. By utilizing online job search engines, social media, and local businesses, teens can find part-time job and internship opportunities that align with their interests and goals. Part-time jobs and internships can lead to successful outcomes such as professional development, college applications, and long-term career opportunities.

Some information where students aspire to go to college are as follows:

The Indian Institutes of Technology (IITs) are some of the most prestigious engineering colleges in India, and are known for their rigorous academic programs and competitive entrance exams.

The Jawaharlal Nehru University (JNU) in Delhi is known for its social science and humanities programs, and is considered one of the top universities in India.

The Indian government launched the Rashtriya Uchchatar Shiksha Abhiyan (RUSA) in 2013, which aims to improve the quality of higher education in India by providing funding to colleges and universities.

The Indian Institute of Management (IIM) is a group of 20 premier management colleges in India that offer postgraduate programs in management and business administration.

The University Grants Commission (UGC) is the regulatory body responsible for maintaining the standards of higher education in India.

CHAPTER THIRTEEN

Investing in the Stock Market

Investing is a great way to build wealth over time. In this chapter, we'll explore the benefits of investing in the stock market, how to get started, and the risks involved.

Benefits of Investing in the Stock Market: Investing in the stock market can be a great way to grow your money over time. Here are some of the key benefits:

Compound Interest: One of the most significant benefits of investing in the stock market is the power of compound interest. When you invest in stocks, you earn returns on your investment. Over time, those returns can earn returns of their own, creating a snowball effect that can lead to significant gains.

Diversification: Investing in the stock market allows you to diversify your portfolio. By investing in different types of stocks, you spread your risk across multiple investments, reducing the impact of any one company's performance.

Long-Term Growth: While the stock market can be volatile in the short-term, over the long-term, it has historically provided solid returns. By investing in the stock market, you're investing in the future growth of the economy, which can lead to significant gains over time.

Getting Started: Before you invest in the stock market, there are a few things you need to know.

Understand Your Risk Tolerance: Investing in the stock market involves risk. Before you invest, you need to understand your risk tolerance and how much you're willing to lose.

Start Small: You don't need to invest a large sum of money to get started. Begin with a small amount and gradually increase your investment over time.

Do Your Research: Before you invest in a company, do your research. Look at the company's financial statements, earnings reports, and analyst reports to get a sense of its performance and potential for growth.

Risks of Not Investing: While investing in the stock market involves risk, not investing can also be risky. Here are some of the key risks of not investing:

Inflation: Over time, the cost of goods and services increases due to inflation. If your money is sitting in a savings account, it's not earning enough to keep up with inflation, and you're losing purchasing power.

Missed Opportunities: By not investing, you're missing out on potential gains in the stock market. Over time, those missed gains can add up, leading to a significant opportunity cost.

Shortfall in Retirement: If you don't invest for retirement, you may not have enough money to support yourself when you're no longer working.

If you want to dive deeper into the world of investing in the stock market, be sure to check out my previous book, "Stock Market for Teens." In that book, I provide a more in-depth look at how the stock market works, how to pick stocks, and other investment strategies. With the knowledge gained from "Stock Market for Teens," you'll be well-equipped to start investing and building wealth through the stock market.

Conclusion: Investing in the stock market can be a great way to build wealth over time. By understanding your risk tolerance, starting small, and doing your research, you can make informed decisions and reap the benefits of long-term growth and compound interest. Don't let the fear of risk hold you back from investing in your future. Start today and see the benefits for yourself!

CHAPTER FOURTEEN

Building a Diversified Investment Portfolio

Investing in a diversified portfolio is one of the best ways to reduce risk while maximizing returns. In this chapter, we'll explore the benefits of a diversified investment portfolio, how to build one, and the different types of investments to consider.

Benefits of a Diversified Investment Portfolio: A diversified investment portfolio offers several benefits, including:

Risk Reduction: By investing in different types of assets, you spread your risk across multiple investments, reducing the impact of any one asset's performance.

Increased Returns: A diversified portfolio can lead to increased returns over time. By investing in different assets, you can capture gains from multiple areas of the market.

Flexibility: A diversified portfolio allows you to adjust your investments over time based on changes in the market or your financial situation.

Building a Diversified Investment Portfolio: To build a diversified investment portfolio, follow these steps:

Set Investment Goals: Determine your investment goals, including your risk tolerance, time horizon, and return expectations.

Allocate Your Investments: Allocate your investments across different asset classes, such as stocks, bonds, real estate, and alternative investments.

Rebalance Your Portfolio: Rebalance your portfolio periodically to ensure it stays in line with your investment goals.

Types of Investments to Consider: Here are some of the different types of investments to consider when building a diversified portfolio:

Stocks: Stocks offer long-term growth potential and can be a great way to capture gains from the economy's growth.

Bonds: Bonds provide income and stability to a portfolio and can be an excellent way to diversify away from stocks.

Real Estate: Real estate can provide income and diversification away from traditional assets like stocks and bonds.

Alternative Investments: Alternative investments, such as private equity, hedge funds, and commodities, can offer diversification and growth potential, but often have higher fees and lower liquidity.

Conclusion: Building a diversified investment portfolio is a critical part of long-term investing success. By following the steps outlined in this chapter and investing in different asset classes, you can reduce your risk, increase your returns, and achieve your investment goals. Remember to periodically review and adjust your portfolio to ensure it stays in line with your goals and risk tolerance.

CHAPTER FIFTEEN

Understanding Retirement Planning

Retirement planning might seem like something that's only for adults, but it's never too early to start thinking about your future. In this chapter, we'll explore what retirement planning is, why it's important, and how you can get started.

What is Retirement Planning?

Retirement planning is the process of saving and investing money to ensure a comfortable lifestyle in your golden years. This means having enough money to cover your living expenses and any other activities you may want to pursue after you stop working.

Why is Retirement Planning Important?

Retirement planning is essential for several reasons:

Longer Life Expectancy: People are living longer than ever before, and you want to make sure you have enough money to cover your living expenses during retirement.

The Cost of Living: The cost of living is continually increasing, and you want to make sure your retirement income can keep up with inflation.

No Guarantee of Social Security: While Social Security provides some income during retirement, it's not guaranteed to cover all your living expenses.

How to Get Started with Retirement Planning: Here are some steps you can take to start planning for retirement:

Set Retirement Goals: Determine how much money you'll need during retirement, taking into account your living expenses and other activities you may want to pursue.

Start Saving Early: The earlier you start saving for retirement, the more time your money has to grow.

Invest in Retirement Accounts:

Investing in retirement accounts is an essential part of retirement planning in India. There are several types of retirement accounts available in India, each with its own set of rules and benefits. Here are some of the most popular retirement accounts in India:

Employees' Provident Fund (EPF): The EPF is a government-sponsored retirement savings scheme that is available to all employees who work for an organization with 20 or more employees. Both the employee and the employer contribute to the scheme, and the contributions are tax-free.

Public Provident Fund (PPF): The PPF is a government-sponsored retirement savings scheme that is available to all Indian citizens. Contributions to the PPF are tax-deductible, and the interest earned on the contributions is tax-free.

National Pension System (NPS): The NPS is a government-sponsored pension scheme that is available to all Indian citizens. It allows individuals to contribute towards their retirement savings, and the contributions are invested in various securities such as equities, corporate bonds, and government securities. The NPS offers tax benefits to both the employee and the employer.

Atal Pension Yojana (APY): The APY is a government-sponsored pension scheme that is available to all Indian citizens between the ages of 18 and 40. The scheme provides a fixed pension to the subscriber after they reach the age of 60. The contributions to the APY are tax-deductible.

Investing in retirement accounts in India is a smart way to plan for your future. These accounts offer tax benefits, provide a regular income after retirement, and help you build a corpus for your golden years. It's important to start investing in retirement accounts as early as possible to take advantage of the power of compounding. By doing so, you can ensure a comfortable lifestyle in your retirement years.

Consider Your Risk Tolerance: Determine your risk tolerance, or how much risk you're willing to take on to achieve higher returns.

It would help us if we could determine How Much Will You Need for Retirement? Take a few minutes to think how much money you'll need during retirement.

Compound Interest: Compound interest is your best friend when it comes to retirement planning. The earlier you start saving and investing, the more time your money has to grow through compounding.

Conclusion: Retirement planning might seem like something you don't need to worry about as a teen, but it's never too early to start. By following the steps outlined in this chapter, you can start saving and investing for your future and ensure a comfortable lifestyle in your golden years. Remember to periodically review and adjust your retirement plan to ensure it stays in line with your goals and risk tolerance.

CHAPTER SIXTEEN

Creating an Emergency Fund

Life is unpredictable, and emergencies can happen at any time. These emergencies can include unexpected medical expenses, job loss, car repairs, and other unexpected expenses. Having an emergency fund can help you weather these storms without disrupting your financial stability. In this chapter, we will discuss what an emergency fund is, why it is important to have one, and how you can create one.

What is an Emergency Fund?

An emergency fund is a sum of money that you set aside to use in case of unexpected expenses or emergencies. This fund is separate from your regular savings and should only be used for emergencies. The goal is to have enough money in your emergency fund to cover at least 3-6 months of living expenses.

Why is an Emergency Fund Important?

Having an emergency fund is important for several reasons. First, it provides a safety net in case of unexpected expenses. For example, if your car breaks down and requires expensive repairs, you can use the emergency fund to pay for them instead of putting them on your credit card and accumulating debt.

Second, having an emergency fund can help you avoid financial stress. Knowing that you have a financial cushion can provide peace of mind and reduce stress levels. Third, having an emergency fund can help you avoid dipping into your long-term savings, such as retirement accounts, to pay for unexpected expenses.

How to Create an Emergency Fund?

Creating an emergency fund may seem daunting, but it is actually quite simple. Here are some steps you can follow to create an emergency fund:

Set a Goal: Determine how much money you want to save for your emergency fund. As mentioned earlier, aim to save enough to cover at least 3-6 months of living expenses.

Create a Budget: Review your income and expenses to determine how much money you can allocate towards your emergency fund. Look for areas where you can cut back on expenses to free up more money.

Choose a Savings Account: You should keep your emergency fund in a separate savings account that is easily accessible, but not too easily accessible. This account should be separate from your regular savings account, and ideally, it should be in a different bank altogether.

Make Regular Contributions: Set up automatic contributions from your paycheck or checking account to your emergency fund savings account. Even small contributions on a regular basis can add up over time.

Real-Life Examples:

Let us look at some real-life examples of how an emergency fund can be beneficial:

Example 1: Sarah lost her job unexpectedly and was unable to find a new job for several months. Fortunately, she had an emergency fund that covered her living expenses until she found a new job.

Example 2: Raj's car broke down and required expensive repairs. He was able to pay for the repairs with his emergency fund instead of putting them on his credit card and accumulating debt.

Example 3: Priya's father fell ill and required hospitalization. The medical bills were expensive, but

Priya was able to pay for them with her emergency fund instead of dipping into her long-term savings.

Cons of Failing to Create an Emergency Fund:

Failing to create an emergency fund can have serious consequences. Without an emergency fund, you may have to rely on credit cards, personal loans, or other sources of debt to pay for unexpected expenses. This can lead to high-interest payments and debt accumulation, which can be difficult to pay off.

Conclusion: Creating an emergency fund is an essential part of financial planning. It can help you weather life's unexpected twists and turns without disrupting your financial stability. By setting a goal, creating a budget, choosing a savings account, and making regular contributions, you can create an emergency fund that provides a safety net for you and your family

CHAPTER SEVENTEEN

Entrepreneurship and Starting a Business

Entrepreneurship is an exciting journey that offers endless possibilities for those willing to take risks, work hard, and persevere. Starting a business is not only about making money; it's about pursuing your passion and making a difference in the world. In this chapter, we will discuss entrepreneurship, starting a business, and what it takes to succeed in this field.

What is Entrepreneurship?

Entrepreneurship is the process of starting, managing, and growing a business venture with the goal of making a profit. It involves taking risks, being innovative, and having the ability to see opportunities where others see challenges. Entrepreneurs are risk-takers who are willing to put their ideas and resources on the line to create something new and valuable.

Starting a Business: Starting a business can be a challenging and rewarding experience. Here are some steps you can follow to start your own business:

Identify Your Passion: The first step in starting a business is to identify what you are passionate about. This could be anything from creating a product or service to solving a problem or improving an existing product or service.

Research Your Market: Once you have identified your passion, research your market to determine if there is a need for your product or service. Identify your target audience, their needs, and how you can fulfill those needs.

Create a Business Plan: A business plan is a roadmap for your business that outlines your goals, strategies, and financial projections. It should include a description of your product or service, your target market, your marketing plan, and your financial projections.

Secure Funding: Depending on the type of business you are starting, you may need to secure funding to get started. This could be in the form of a loan, grant, or investment.

Launch Your Business: Once you have secured funding and created a business plan, it's time to launch your business. This involves setting up your website, creating marketing materials, and starting to sell your product or service.

Success Stories: Here are some examples of successful entrepreneurs who started their own businesses:

Steve Jobs - Co-founder of Apple Inc. and creator of the iPhone, iPad, and iPod.

Oprah Winfrey - Media mogul and founder of the Oprah Winfrey Network.

Elon Musk - Founder of SpaceX, Tesla, Neuralink, and The Boring Company.

Mark Zuckerberg - Co-founder of Facebook, the world's largest social media platform.

Failure Stories: Not every entrepreneur succeeds on their first try. Here are some examples of entrepreneurs who faced failure before achieving success:

Walt Disney - Was fired from a newspaper for lacking imagination and started several failed businesses before creating Disney Studios.

Thomas Edison - Failed over 1,000 times before successfully inventing the light bulb.

Colonel Sanders - Was rejected over 1,000 times before successfully franchising KFC.

Traps to Avoid: Here are some common traps that entrepreneurs should avoid:

Not Doing Enough Research: Before starting a business, it's important to do your research and understand your market.

Underestimating Expenses: Many new entrepreneurs underestimate the amount of money it takes to start and run a business.

Focusing Too Much on Perfection: While it's important to strive for quality, perfectionism can lead to delays and missed opportunities.

Learnings from the Greats: Here are some learnings from successful entrepreneurs:

Steve Jobs - Focus on the user experience and make products that people love.

Richard Branson - Take calculated risks and don't be afraid to fail.

Sara Blakely - Embrace failure as a learning opportunity and keep moving forward.

Ritesh Agarwal: Ritesh Agarwal is the founder of OYO Rooms, a budget hotel chain that has disrupted the hospitality industry in India. He started OYO Rooms in 2013 at the age of 19, and within a few years, the company had become a unicorn with a valuation of over $10 billion.

Vijay Shekhar Sharma: Vijay Shekhar Sharma is the founder of Paytm, India's leading mobile payments and financial services company. He started Paytm in 2010, and today, the company has over 450 million users and a valuation of over $16 billion.

Falguni Nayar: Falguni Nayar is the founder of Nykaa, India's leading online beauty retailer. She started Nykaa in 2012, and today, the company has a valuation of over $2 billion. Nayar has been named one of Forbes India's most powerful women entrepreneurs multiple times.

Bhavish Aggarwal: Bhavish Aggarwal is the founder of Ola, India's leading ride-hailing company. He started Ola in 2010 with a few friends, and today, the company has over 1 million drivers across 250 cities in India. Ola is now expanding to other markets, including Australia and the UK.

These entrepreneurs have shown that with hard work, perseverance, and a willingness to take risks, anyone can start and grow a successful business.

Start:

Starting a business can be daunting, but it all starts with an idea. Once you have a business idea, the next step is to do some market research to see if there is a demand for your product or service. This could include surveying potential customers or looking at similar businesses in your area to see if there is room for a new player in the market.

Once you have done your research, it's time to create a business plan. A business plan is a roadmap that outlines your goals, target market, marketing strategy, financial projections, and more. It's important to have a solid plan in place before launching your business.

Crawl:

Now that you have a plan in place, it's time to start building a strong foundation for your business. This could include:

Refining your product or service: Make sure your product or service is the best it can be before launching. This could mean conducting product tests or getting feedback from potential customers.

Building a website: A website is a must-have for any business in today's digital age. Make sure your website is user-friendly and showcases your product or service in the best possible light.

Creating marketing materials: Once you have a website, it's time to start promoting your business. This could include creating social media accounts, designing flyers, or running ads on platforms like Google or Facebook.

Run:

Once you have a solid foundation in place, it's time to start growing your business. This could include:

Expanding your product or service offerings: If your business is successful, consider expanding your product or service offerings to appeal to a wider audience.

Hiring employees: As your business grows, you may need to hire employees to help you manage the workload. Make sure you hire people who are a good fit for your company culture and have the necessary skills to help your business succeed.

Scaling your marketing efforts: Once you have a marketing strategy in place, it's time to scale your efforts to reach even more customers. This could include running ads on television or radio, hosting events, or partnering with other businesses to cross-promote.

Fly:

Once your business is successful and has a strong reputation in the market, it's time to start thinking about scaling and taking your business to the next level. This could include:

Expanding to new markets: If your business is successful in one location, consider expanding to new markets. This could be in the form of opening new locations or launching an e-commerce store to reach customers across the globe.

Diversifying your offerings: As your business grows, consider diversifying your offerings to reduce risk and appeal to a wider audience. This could include launching a new product line or offering new services.

Innovating: Innovation is key to staying ahead of the competition. Keep an eye on emerging trends and technologies and be willing to pivot your business to stay relevant in a rapidly changing market.

Starting a business is not easy, but with hard work, perseverance, and a solid plan in place, it is possible to succeed. Remember to start small, focus on building a strong foundation, and never stop learning and innovating.

CHAPTER EIGHTEEN

Managing Risk and Insurance

When it comes to personal finance, managing risk is an important aspect that should not be ignored. Risk is a part of life, and it is essential to have a plan in place to manage it effectively. One of the best ways to manage risk is through insurance. In this chapter, we will discuss the types of insurance, their importance, what to avoid, and what happens if you fail to buy insurance.

Types of Insurance:

Insurance is a contract between the insured (the person who is buying insurance) and the insurer (the company selling insurance). In exchange for a premium (the amount paid to the insurer), the insurer agrees to pay the insured in the event of a covered loss. Here are the most common types of insurance:

Life Insurance: Life insurance is a type of insurance that provides financial security to the family in the event of the policyholder's death. The policyholder pays a premium, and in return, the insurance company provides a lump sum payment to the beneficiary upon the policyholder's death.

Let's say, for example, that your parents have taken out a life insurance policy on themselves. If something were to happen to them, the insurance company would pay out a lump sum to you or your siblings. This money could be used to cover the costs of the funeral, pay off any outstanding debts, or provide financial support for the family.

Health Insurance: Health insurance is a type of insurance that covers the cost of medical treatment. It can help to cover the cost of hospitalization, surgery, and other medical expenses.

Health insurance is especially important in today's world, where medical expenses can be astronomical. If you were to get seriously ill or injured, having health insurance could mean the difference between getting the treatment you need and going bankrupt.

Auto Insurance: Auto insurance is a type of insurance that covers the cost of damages or injuries that you may cause in a car accident.

Auto insurance is a legal requirement in many places, and for good reason. Car accidents can be costly affairs, and if you were to cause one, you could be on the hook for damages and injuries that could be financially devastating. Auto insurance helps to protect you from these potential financial losses.

Importance of Insurance:

Insurance is important because it helps to protect you from financial risks that are beyond your control. Whether it's a serious illness, a car accident, or the death of a loved one, insurance can help to provide financial security when you need it most.

One of the biggest advantages of insurance is that it can help to mitigate risk. By paying a relatively small premium, you can transfer the risk of a potentially catastrophic event to an insurance company. This can give you peace of mind and help to protect your financial future.

What to Avoid:

When it comes to buying insurance, there are a few things that you should avoid. Here are some of the most common mistakes that people make when buying insurance:

Not shopping around: Insurance is a competitive industry, and there are often many different options available. By shopping around and comparing prices, you can often find a better deal than if you were to go with the first insurer you come across.

Not understanding the terms and conditions: Insurance policies can be complex documents, and it's important to read them carefully before signing up. Make sure you understand what is covered and what is not, as well as any limits or exclusions that may apply.

Underinsuring: While it's tempting to try to save money on insurance premiums, underinsuring can be a costly mistake. If you don't have enough coverage, you could end up having to pay out of pocket for expenses that are not covered by your policy.

Choosing the right insurance policy for your needs can be overwhelming. To simplify the process, you can use the following tips:

Determine your needs: The first step in choosing the right insurance policy is to determine what type of coverage you need. For example, if you are a car owner, you need to have car insurance. If you have dependents, you need life insurance. If you own a house, you need homeowners insurance. Once you have identified your needs, you can then begin to research the different insurance options available to you.

Shop around: When it comes to insurance, it pays to shop around. Different insurance providers offer different policies and rates, so it is important to compare multiple options before making a decision. You can use online comparison tools or work with an insurance broker to get quotes from multiple providers.

Read the fine print: Before signing on the dotted line, make sure you read the fine print of your policy. Pay close attention to the coverage limits, deductibles, exclusions, and other important details. If there is anything you don't understand, ask your insurance provider for clarification.

Consider the cost: While cost should not be the only factor you consider when choosing an insurance policy, it is an important one. Make sure you choose a policy that is within your budget and offers good value for money.

Review your policy regularly: Your insurance needs can change over time, so it is important to review your policy regularly to ensure it still meets your needs. If you have any major life changes, such as getting married, having a child, or buying a new car, you may need to update your policy

What happens if you don't buy insurance:

Choosing not to buy insurance can have serious consequences in the event of an unexpected incident. In this section, we'll explore what can happen if you fail to buy insurance.

Financial Losses: The most obvious consequence of not having insurance is that you will have to bear the full financial burden of any damages or losses that occur. Depending on the nature of the incident, this could result in thousands or even millions of dollars in costs. For example, if you are involved in a car accident and do not have auto insurance, you will be responsible for paying for any damages to your own vehicle, as well as any damages or injuries caused to the other party.

Legal Troubles: In some cases, failing to have insurance can also result in legal troubles. For example, if you are involved in a car accident and do not have auto insurance, you may be fined or even face criminal charges.

Difficulty Getting Coverage Later: Another consequence of not having insurance is that it may become more difficult to get coverage in the future. Insurance providers may see you as a high-risk individual and charge you higher premiums or deny you coverage altogether.

Difficulty Managing Risk: Without insurance, you are also at a greater risk of financial ruin in the event of a disaster. This can make it difficult to manage risk and plan for the future.

Missed Opportunities: Finally, failing to have insurance can also result in missed opportunities. For example, if you do not have health insurance, you may be unable to take advantage of preventative care or screenings that could help you detect and treat health issues early.

In conclusion, failing to buy insurance can have serious consequences. By taking steps to protect yourself against unforeseen events, you can safeguard your financial future and enjoy greater peace of mind.

Managing risk and insurance is an important part of personal finance. By understanding the different types of insurance available, and taking steps to protect yourself against unforeseen events, you can safeguard your financial future and enjoy greater peace of mind.

CHAPTER NINETEEN

Making Financial Decisions as an Adult

Making financial decisions as an adult can be both exciting and overwhelming. On one hand, you have the freedom to make your own choices and take control of your finances. On the other hand, you are now responsible for managing your own money and making decisions that will impact your future. In this chapter, we'll explore some tips and strategies for making smart financial decisions as a young adult.

Set Financial Goals: The first step in making smart financial decisions is to set clear and measurable goals. This could include saving for a down payment on a house, paying off student loans, or starting a retirement fund. By having specific goals in mind, you can create a plan to achieve them and stay motivated along the way.

Create a Budget: Creating a budget is another important step in making smart financial decisions. A budget helps you track your income and expenses and identify areas where you can cut back and save money. To create a budget, start by tracking your expenses for a month and categorizing them into different areas such as housing, transportation, food, and entertainment. Then, set realistic spending limits for each category and stick to them.

Build a Strong Credit History: Your credit history is an important factor in many financial decisions, including getting approved for loans, renting an apartment, and even getting a job. To build a strong credit history, make sure to pay your bills on time, keep your credit card balances low, and avoid applying for too much credit at once.

Understand Taxes: Taxes can be confusing, but it's important to understand how they work and how they impact your finances. Make sure to familiarize yourself with the different types of taxes you may have to pay, such as income tax and sales tax, and learn about any deductions or credits you may be eligible for.

Seek Professional Advice: If you're feeling overwhelmed or unsure about a financial decision, don't be afraid to seek professional advice. This could include speaking with a financial advisor, accountant, or lawyer. These professionals can provide valuable guidance and help you make informed decisions about your finances.

Take Calculated Risks: Finally, it's important to take calculated risks when it comes to your finances. This could include investing in the stock market, starting a business, or pursuing a higher education degree. However, it's important to do your research and make sure you understand the potential risks and rewards before making a decision.

Understanding credit scores: As teens start to enter adulthood, they may start building their credit score. It's important to understand what a credit score is and how it impacts your ability to borrow money. You can explain the concept of credit scores in simple terms and provide tips on how to maintain a good score.

Avoiding debt traps: As young adults start earning, they may be tempted to indulge in unnecessary expenses and buy things they can't afford. This can lead to a debt trap, where they end up paying high-interest rates on their loans. You can provide tips on how to avoid falling into a debt trap, such as creating a budget, living below your means, and avoiding unnecessary expenses.

Saving for retirement: It's never too early to start saving for retirement. You can explain the benefits of starting early and compounding interest. You can also explain different retirement plans like PF,NPS and how they work.

Building an emergency fund: An emergency fund is important to have in case of unexpected events like job loss, medical expenses, or a sudden financial crisis. You can explain the importance of having an emergency fund and provide tips on how to build one.

Investing for long-term goals: Investing is important to achieve long-term financial goals like buying a house, starting a business, or retiring early. You can provide an overview of different investment options like stocks, bonds, mutual funds, and real estate. You can also explain the risks and benefits of each option.

Seeking professional advice: As teens become adults, they may face complex financial decisions that require professional advice. You can explain the benefits of seeking professional advice and how to find a trusted financial advisor.

In conclusion, making smart financial decisions as an adult requires careful planning, budgeting, and a willingness to seek advice when needed. By following these tips and strategies, you can take control of your finances and build a strong financial future. And remember, while it's important to be responsible with your money, it's also okay to have a little fun and enjoy the journey along the way.

CHAPTER TWENTY

Tips for Long-Term Financial Success

Start early: As we discussed earlier, starting early can make a huge difference in your financial success. The earlier you start, the more time your money has to grow. Think of it like planting a seed that grows into a big tree over time.

Live below your means: It's tempting to spend all your money as soon as you earn it, but it's important to live below your means. This means spending less than you earn so you can save and invest for the future. You can have fun and enjoy life without overspending.

Create a budget: A budget is a plan that helps you track your income and expenses. Creating a budget can help you understand where your money is going and make adjustments if necessary. You can make budgeting fun by using colorful charts or apps to track your expenses.

Save for big purchases: Instead of taking out loans or credit cards to buy big-ticket items, start saving for them in advance. This can help you avoid high-interest rates and debt traps. You can make saving fun by setting up a savings jar or a goal tracker.

Avoid debt: Debt can be a trap that keeps you from achieving your financial goals. Avoid taking on unnecessary debt, like credit card debt or high-interest loans. You can make avoiding debt fun by challenging yourself to find creative ways to save money, like packing your own lunch or taking public transportation.

Invest for the future: Investing can help your money grow over time and reach your long-term financial goals. Start by investing in low-cost index funds or mutual funds, and avoid risky investments that promise high returns. You can make investing fun by learning about different investment options and tracking your progress.

Seek financial advice: Finally, don't be afraid to seek advice from trusted financial experts. They can help you understand complex financial concepts and make informed decisions. You can make seeking advice fun by finding a mentor or attending financial education events.

By following these tips and taking control of their finances, teens can set themselves up for long-term financial success. Remember, financial success doesn't have to be boring – it can be fun and exciting!

It's true that some of these tips may seem repetitive or common sense, but it's important to remember that repetition is the key to success. Building good financial habits takes time and effort, and it's easy to slip into bad habits if we don't consistently reinforce positive ones.

Repeating these tips and implementing them into your daily life can help make them second nature. You may find yourself naturally living below your means, sticking to a budget, and saving for the future without even thinking about it.

In addition, it's important to remember that while some of these tips may seem basic, they are crucial for building a strong financial foundation. Skipping any of these steps can lead to financial stress, debt, and missed opportunities for growth and wealth building.

By taking the time to build good financial habits now, teens can set themselves up for a lifetime of financial success. So even though some of these tips may seem repetitive or basic, they are worth implementing and repeating until they become habits. It's never too early (or late) to start building a strong financial future!

CHAPTER TWENTY-ONE

Real Life cautionary tales.

The last chapter of this book "Personal Finance for Teens" discusses cautionary tales from real life examples of individuals who have experienced financial success and failure.

One such example is the story of Baba Ka Dhaba, a small eatery in Delhi that gained nationwide attention and support during the COVID-19 pandemic.

Baba Ka Dhaba was a small food stall run by an elderly couple who struggled to make ends meet. One day, a customer posted a video of the couple on social media, which went viral, leading to an outpouring of support from the community and media. As a result, the couple's business saw a massive surge in customers and revenue, and they became overnight sensations. However, their newfound success did not last long. The couple was unable to manage their finances effectively, and they quickly fell back into financial difficulty, eventually losing their business and all the goodwill they had gained.

After the viral video and the massive surge in customers and revenue, Baba Ka Dhaba initially seemed to be doing well. However, they were not prepared for the sudden increase in demand and were unable to manage their finances effectively. They started spending more money than they were making, assuming that the good times would continue.

The couple also faced several challenges in managing their business. They were not accustomed to the sudden fame and attention they were receiving and did not have the necessary resources or support to handle it all. They had difficulty hiring additional staff to keep up with the demand and were unable to source fresh ingredients consistently. These challenges made it difficult for them to maintain the quality of their food and meet the expectations of their customers.

As a result of these challenges, Baba Ka Dhaba's customer base started to dwindle, and their revenue began to decline. The couple had also accumulated significant debt, which they were unable to repay. They had invested a lot of money in the business, including hiring additional staff and buying expensive equipment. However, they were not generating enough revenue to cover these costs and were quickly falling into financial difficulty.

The situation became worse when the couple got into a legal dispute with the owner of the property where their stall was located. They were asked to vacate the premises, and they had to find a new location to run their business. This added further expenses and stress to their already precarious financial situation.

Eventually, the couple was forced to shut down their business, and they lost everything they had gained during their brief period of fame. They were unable to pay off their debts, and their reputation suffered a severe blow. The couple had no other source of income and were forced to rely on donations from well-wishers and the community.

Baba Ka Dhaba's story serves as a cautionary tale for anyone starting a business. While sudden success can be tempting, it is crucial to be prepared for it and have a solid financial plan in place. Managing cash flow, controlling expenses, and maintaining quality are essential to sustaining a business in the long run. Baba Ka Dhaba's downfall was a result of their inability to manage their finances effectively and respond to the challenges they faced. Their story is a reminder that even a moment of viral fame can be fleeting, and it is important to have a plan for the future to avoid falling back into financial difficulty.

This story highlights the importance of financial literacy and proper management of finances, even when experiencing unexpected success. It is essential to have a solid financial plan in place to manage unexpected gains or windfalls, to avoid overspending and falling back into financial difficulty.

The story of Baba Ka Dhaba also demonstrates the power of social media and the impact it can have on small businesses. By using social media platforms to promote their business and engage with their customers, small businesses can gain valuable exposure and build a loyal customer base. However, it is also important to be prepared for sudden spikes in demand and to have a plan in place to manage cash flow and expenses.

In conclusion, the cautionary tale of Baba Ka Dhaba provides valuable lessons for anyone starting a business or managing their finances. It is essential to have a solid financial plan, be prepared for unexpected events, and use social media and other tools effectively to grow and manage your business. With these principles in mind, anyone can achieve financial success and avoid the pitfalls of financial mismanagement.

Sushil Kumar is another example of how sudden fame and fortune can lead to financial downfall if not managed correctly. Sushil Kumar is a former government clerk from a small village in Bihar who participated in the game show Kaun Banega Crorepati and won 5 crores ($1 million) in prize money. Like Baba Ka Dhaba, Sushil Kumar became an overnight sensation, with media outlets hailing him as a hero and an inspiration to millions.

However, Sushil Kumar was unable to manage his newfound wealth effectively. He made several poor financial decisions, including investing in a movie that flopped and buying a house in a neighborhood that was far beyond his means. He also faced pressure from friends and family members who asked for loans and financial assistance, which further drained his savings.

As a result of these poor financial decisions, Sushil Kumar quickly fell back into financial difficulty. He was unable to pay his bills, and his debts started to pile up. He also faced legal troubles when he was unable to pay his taxes and was forced to sell his assets to pay off his debts. Eventually, Sushil Kumar lost everything he had gained from his appearance on the show and was forced to return to his old job as a government clerk to make ends meet.

After winning the prize money of 5 crores ($1 million) on Kaun Banega Crorepati, Sushil Kumar made some poor financial decisions that quickly led to his downfall. One of his first mistakes was investing a significant portion of his winnings in a movie that turned out to be a commercial failure. This loss was a significant blow to his finances, and it set him on a path of financial ruin.

Sushil Kumar also made the mistake of buying a house in a posh locality in Delhi, which was far beyond his means. He took out a loan to finance the purchase and was unable to make the monthly payments on time. He faced a lot of stress from the bank and was ultimately forced to sell the house at a loss to pay off his debt.

Another mistake Sushil Kumar made was lending money to his friends and family members who were facing financial difficulties. He did not have the expertise or experience to manage his finances effectively and was unable to assess the risks involved in lending money to his loved ones. This led to further financial stress and put a significant strain on his relationship with his friends and family.

To make matters worse, Sushil Kumar also faced legal trouble when he was unable to pay his taxes on time. The government seized his assets, including his car, to recover the unpaid taxes, further adding to his financial difficulties. He was unable to pay his bills and fell into debt, forcing him to sell his assets to pay off his creditors.

Despite all his struggles, Sushil Kumar never lost hope and continued to work hard to make ends meet. He took up odd jobs and worked as a clerk in a government office to support himself and his family. He also tried his hand at politics, but his lack of experience and knowledge in the field made it difficult for him to succeed.

Sushil Kumar's story serves as a cautionary tale for anyone who experiences sudden wealth. It is essential to manage your finances effectively and make informed decisions about how to invest your money. Seeking the advice of financial experts and professionals can help you make better decisions and avoid financial ruin. Sushil Kumar's experience also highlights the importance of financial literacy and education to empower individuals to make better financial decisions and avoid falling into debt and financial ruin.

The stories of Baba Ka Dhaba and Sushil Kumar highlight the importance of financial literacy and proper management of finances, even when experiencing unexpected success. It is easy to become complacent and assume that the good times will continue, but it is essential to have a solid financial plan in place to manage sudden gains or windfalls effectively.

Some key takeaways from these cautionary tales include:

Have a solid financial plan in place: This includes creating a budget, saving money, and investing in a diversified portfolio.

Be prepared for sudden changes: Fame and fortune can be fleeting, and it is important to have a plan for the future and to be prepared for unexpected events.

Avoid making impulsive financial decisions: It is easy to get carried away with the excitement of newfound wealth, but it is important to make thoughtful and strategic decisions about how to manage your money.

Seek professional advice: If you are unsure about how to manage your finances effectively, seek the advice of a financial advisor or accountant who can help you make informed decisions.

In conclusion, the cautionary tales of Baba Ka Dhaba and Sushil Kumar illustrate how sudden success can quickly turn into financial difficulty if not managed correctly. These stories serve as a reminder of the importance of financial literacy and responsible financial management, even in the face of unexpected success.

Here are a few more examples of Indian celebrities who fell into financial difficulty due to poor financial management:

Leander Paes: The Indian tennis player, who has won numerous Grand Slam titles, faced financial difficulties due to a series of poor investments. He invested in a real estate project that never took off, which left him with significant debts. He also faced legal trouble when he was unable to pay his taxes and was forced to sell his assets to repay his creditors.

Dino Morea: The Bollywood actor, who rose to fame in the 2000s, faced financial difficulties due to a string of failed investments. He invested heavily in a chain of restaurants, which failed to generate the expected returns. He was also unable to repay a loan he had taken to finance the restaurants, which led to legal trouble and further financial stress.

Shweta Basu Prasad: The child actor, who won a National Award for her role in the film Makdee, fell into financial difficulty in her adult years. She invested in a business venture that failed and was unable to repay the loans she had taken to finance the project. She was also unable to find work in the film industry, which further added to her financial stress.

Indian cricketer Sreesanth: The Indian cricketer, who was banned from cricket due to a spot-fixing scandal, faced financial difficulty after losing his source of income. He invested in a business venture that failed and was unable to repay the loans he had taken to finance the project. He also faced legal trouble when he was unable to pay his taxes, which added to his financial stress.

Indian cricketer Vinod Kambli. Kambli was one of the most talented cricketers of his time, with a successful international career in the 1990s. However, he was unable to manage his finances effectively and made several poor financial decisions, including investing in a restaurant that failed and buying a lavish house that he could not afford. He also faced legal trouble when he was unable to pay his taxes and was forced to sell his assets to pay off his debts. Eventually, Kambli was left with nothing and had to start from scratch.

Another example is the actor and politician Govinda. Govinda was a highly successful actor in the 1990s, with a massive fan following and a string of successful films. However, he was unable to manage his finances effectively and made several poor financial decisions, including investing in a film that failed and buying a house that was far beyond his means. He also faced legal trouble when he was unable to pay his taxes and was forced to sell his assets to pay off his debts. Govinda was left with no choice but to take up lesser-known roles and work hard to rebuild his career and finances.

These examples illustrate the importance of financial literacy and responsible financial management, even for successful celebrities. It is essential to have a solid financial plan in place and to make informed decisions about investments and expenses to avoid falling into financial difficulty. Seeking professional advice and education in financial management can also help avoid financial ruin.

"building A Strong Financial Future: Your Personal Finance Guide For Life"

Congratulations on finishing "Personal Finance for Teens"! We hope you found this book informative, interesting, and most importantly, helpful for building a strong financial foundation for your future.

Remember, personal finance is a journey, not a destination. Building good financial habits takes time and effort, and it's never too early (or late) to start. The tips and strategies outlined in this book can help you take control of your finances, live below your means, and work towards achieving your financial goals.

Sharing this book, "Personal Finance for Teens," is important because financial literacy is essential for success in life. By learning the basics of personal finance early on, teens can avoid making costly mistakes that can impact their financial future for years to come. With the right guidance, they can learn how to budget their money, save for their future, and invest wisely.

This book is particularly valuable because it is written specifically for youngsters. The language is clear and accessible, and the examples used are relevant to their lives. By making personal finance education fun and engaging, this book encourages teens to take an active role in their financial future and helps them build the confidence they need to make informed financial decisions.

Sharing this book is also important because financial literacy is not taught in many schools, leaving many young people at a disadvantage when it comes to managing their money. By sharing this book with your friends, family, and community, you can help fill this gap and empower the next generation of young people to take control of their finances and build a strong financial future.

In short, by sharing this book, you can help ensure that more young people have the tools they need to succeed in life. With the right knowledge and skills, they can build a solid financial foundation and enjoy a lifetime of financial security and success.

We encourage you to take action and apply what you have learned in this book. Don't be afraid to make mistakes - they can be valuable learning experiences that help you grow and improve. And most importantly, don't be afraid to ask for help or advice from trusted sources.

We wish you all the best on your personal finance journey, and we hope that the knowledge and skills you have gained from this book will serve you well for many years to come.

Sincerely,

Sachin Bansode